AF359158

ANGUISH ABOUND

VALSA JOSEPH

Become Shakespeare
.com

First published in 2022 by
BecomeShakespeare.com

One Point Six Technologies Pvt Ltd.
119-123, 1st Floor, Building J2, B - Wing, WadalaTruck Terminal,
Wadala East, Mumbai, Maharashtra, India, 400022.
T:+91 8080226699

Copyright © 2022 by Valsa Joseph

All rights reserved. Any unauthorized reprint or use of this material is
prohibited. No part of this book may be reproduced or transmitted in any
form or by any means, electronic or mechanical, including photocopying,
recording, or by any information storage and retrieval system without
express written permission from the author/publisher.

Please do not participate in or encourage piracy of copyrighted materials
in violation of the author's rights. Purchase only
authorized editions.

ISBN: 978-93-5610-868-4

INTRODUCTION

The impacts of one's painful experiences last one's life although. They often reflect in thinking, and reacting to the situations around unaware and unconscious. Sons inherit father's names, surnames and riches, so too the bad temperaments often. Wrath is a deadly sin that is transmitted through genes to progeny. Just as the inherited wealth is accumulated the venomous wrath too in many cases. Anyway generalization is not always correct as there are exceptions and variations based on severity and depth of the wounds inflicted on the sufferers and their mental set up to devour or munch them. At times we see vagabonds becoming efficient profit-reaping businessmen and oppressed ones into well known or notorious politicians but sad to say not intellectuals.

Harsh parenting, verbal or physical threats, frequent yellings, rebukings and hittings give way to behavioural issues such as aggressiveness and not following directions at school. According to Dr. Kenneth Ginsburg parents should be lighthouses for their children. Parents more often fathers are toxic:- extremely controlling, highly critical and wanting in empathy. "Geniuses are not often gifted. They are sometimes cursed". This is said of Napoleon Bonaparte. This   is applicable to many a man like my prominent character here. Hitler had very unfortunate boyhood badly beaten and verbally abused everyday, it is remarked. I understand that Francis Lucas had no better boyhood, teenage or youth. He and his mother had always sighs and pants. Like the phoenix a few rise above all miseries and reach heights but many drown in abject misery. Offensive and arrogant parenting is very seldom now a days. It has taken a turn over to overpampering which leads some times to addictions and resultant ruin. Who is able to do perfect or faultless parenting, how many are satisfied or happy about the parenting given or received!!???.`

ABOUT THE AUTHOR

Born in 1947, in Kerala, India in the month of August just 9 days prior to my native land securing independence from Great Britain. I had a married life of 45 years, as common even to this day as an arranged one (be sure not a made one)and have three grown-up children. Though a member of a pretty large family and faced many hardships made my own way to live with hardly any support from without, making full use of the opportunities that knocked at my door for education and securing jobs in different parts of my country and two countries abroad that furnished me with some ideas, understanding, and knowledge of the places and people. It took me nine months for the completion of this book.

I am a US citizen, was in Ethiopia for three years as a teacher and in England for three visits of short time. I was also lucky enough to be in Canada for a short while and Keywest the beautiful island for a visit.

CONTENTS

CHAPTER 1

I, Thomas Joseph have an aptitude for counselling profession. So I am a counsellor. Even in my teenage I had an innate capacity to settle the disputes in my friend circle. Everyone would happily accept my logical arguments and opinion and my confidence in my talent grew by and by. So after schooling I opted psychology for my higher studies in the university. All through my studies I came across people's personal, social and family issues and problems and how all this amounts to the moulding of one's character and life and thus gave me an insight into the reasons for the disorders and discordances in different people's lives. Even after knowing and understanding these facts am I a good family man bestowing happiness to all the members in the family!. I doubt! Life is that. The ultimate meaning of life is that. A tolerably good and tolerably bad one is good enough. So have no notion that a counsellor has extraordinarily smooth life. Only a low percentage of counsellors are well remunerated and so many find tough time making the two ends meet. I had undergone this crisis for a long time till I became a noted one in my profession when my wants and demands were very little apart from medical treatments. All through my career life I enjoyed my profession and took immense pleasure in consoling and guiding my clients not levying fees unaffordable. Very often my pleasure after settling the problems was not long lived. To me and such clients 'full moon' and 'new moon' were periodical visitors but some were permanently swinging in spring, some in perpetual winter. Life is that.

Francis Lucas was a frequent visitor and client of mine all through his teenage, youth and middle age. His experiences and endurances were manifold, quite uncommon and his revelations aroused my hate and sympathy for him and his father.

Pity and sympathy for him,

Painful boyhood, teens and youth,

Crest- fallen and dethroned,

Ego trampled under feet

Like crushed dragon's head

Rebellion aroused as recourse

Resultant middle age abominable,

Self made and inflicted

      Any mother's soul is sorrowful unto grave

      Her veins and marrows know that,

      Toes to skull agony escalates

      Burns often as pain blamed

      Sighs and pants desolate

      Subtle and poise was he,

      Crually smashed and stamped

      Yet, will be recovered one day

      Deep do I believe.

That will be the locus of any mother.

Each incident that Francis Lucas narrated to me is still in my memory. All were such strange and beyond belief. The incidents that Francis shared with me are and will be printed in my brain all the time and work as an instruction to me in guiding my clients and patients.

"You become a Man the day your father dies"

"You are not really an adult until your father dies"

"A boy never really becomes a man until he's buried his   father"

"A boy never becomes a Man until his father dies"

All this point to the fact a boy's personality and ego are often injured by a father and become unbearable and intolerable to the son.

May be these sayings don't much apply now-a-days. Some ten decades ago they applied to many, seven decades ago may be to a fewer ones and four decades ago to still fewer. The haughty and unbecoming pride of men who adorned the status of fathers made them cruel towards their sons inflicting corporal punishments coupled with inhuman and arrogant words and advices. May be such fathers inherited the violent dealings and treatments from their fathers or their self created capricious, venomous views or rather sins that crush and ruin the sons' lives. Such men neither deserve nor receive love from their offsprings and spouses. Such fathers are jealous of the abilities of the sons and their hate leads to disastrous lives of their sons. When any parent quenches his pride and arrogance he is sprouting the same vices in his son. Again it all depends. Some perceive the adverse effects and go to the other end and become real good friends and go on very smooth inviting every onlooker's envy. Some egocentric parents utilize the efforts of their altruistic kids, take advantage of their self denying nature for the benefits of the family and then simply trash them in the garbage bin when they look favourably on their younger kids who are their favourites. Those who experience that may turn reverse and totally never expect anything from their offsprings and return even a gift with more excelling handout. In short some give only, some take only there is indubitably median and mid. I enjoy being in give only status. Such ones strive and struggle till the end and last breath, yet piously self assured. Even then the recollection of laxity and disregard felt and experienced linger with prickings.

Let me be back to Francis Lucas who is still under the yoke of childhood, boyhood and youth affronted and snubbed. I'm sure Francis is awaking, rising and brandishing. He talks to me with envy and appreciation about his cousins and friends who were and are treated as friends by their fathers. His father was one with only a single emotion of anger. Never had he a shadow of love, anxiety or sadness. Yet he was nice enough to perform his duties and responsibilities. According to Francis his father's dealings, reproaches and cruelties made him strong enough to face any difficult situation but this remark did not work out practically. He compared his father to a chippie in an Indian legend who conspired himself to kill his son who was against his father's stringent social norms. The chippie's jealousy towards his offspring's fame, name and respect made him murder his son by dropping his chisel on the latter's neck while they were working together. That was Francis's understanding, rating and judgement of his father. "As is the father so is the son". The application of this is seen in a notable number of sons and Francis is one of the top in the list. He repeatedly says that-

'Dad was not fair to me, he was very cruel towards me all through. I was not good too- I could not be how could I be when I was the sufferer everyday (no exaggeration) I had to react to survive'.

* * *

CHAPTER 2

It was a Saturday by 11am. That was my first acquaintance with Francis. As soon as he entered my consulting room the four eyes met for a few seconds without any wink followed by cordial smiles on both their lips and amicable facial expressions. I directed the youngster to the patient chair by my palm gesture and a slight nod of the head with an eye contact. He took his seat and our eyes met again. Turning pale and embarrassed he sat staring at the floor. He pulled himself together and took the initiative to break the silence, introducing himself to me. Under such delicate situations usually the psychologist comes out with simple and casual talk to encourage the patient to speak out. Thus at the very outset Francis proved to me that he was a notably bold me. I wanted to promote his gutsy. Dr. Thomas Joseph, "you are something and you will be more, I am more than sure. Open up have no fears." This made Francis summon up all his courage. He eyed his doctor and the latter caught the former's eye and tossed his head in encouragement.

'Doctor, I was fourteen then and am seventeen now. My hair stood on end always when near my father. We had and have quite a big cow shed wide enough for 5 to 6 and their heifers and claves. We live in a village fifteen kilometers from the big town. All the inhabitants are typical villagers leading simple lives having rubber plantations small or big, cultivating commercial crops like coconut palms, cocoa plants, ginger, turmeric and so on. Our house is only ten minutes walk from the Periyar river the other side of which is the forest thick and dark with the lush and ampleness of teak trees. Rearing cows is done on small scale by the majority of the people here, as the cattle are trained to swim across the river and graze in the forest. Only rarely it happens that any stay back in the forest and eaten by tiger. Sometimes I go or am sent to the river bank to bring the cattle home. One day it happened that I returned home very late, even then before the sun hid behind the horizon bringing the cows. Dad and I fastened them each to its spot. He was holding the cow's rope in his hand and reached me asking why I was that late. I was tongue-tied seeing his fury on the face and the rope in the hand. Like a docile and humble son I told him.

Dad, all my friends were in the playground watching and playing cricket and I too joined them."

My pleading look and scared and sad gesture had no influence on his ghastly countenance at all. He mercilessly whipped me with the double folded rope several times and then went his way. I had terrible pain and pricking and burning sensation in my skin. Hearing my cries and sobs my mother ran to me consoling, comforting and sympathizing. Tears dropped down her eyes when she caught sight of the marks and stains left on my legs. She applied and rubbed some pain balm on the bruises to heal and sooth.

Doctor, "Francis, let me ask you a question. Does your dad take alcohol often?."

"He never drinks or smokes, yet he is not a good family man as he ill treats me, torments me physically and mentally and torments my mum mentally and penetrates unhappiness in the family."

Doctor "Sorry for the interruption. Carry on"

Francis "No problem doctor, it was a reasonable and relevant question throwing light on his personality. Back to my narration. My anger, repugnance and revenge overshadowed my physical pain and mental anguish. I was not clear in my mind what I was upto. Opening the gate of our house and yard I just walked out aimless. Though I heard my mother calling me, ignoring it I walked away. The sun was punctual in effectuating its routine function hiding behind the horizon putting some to slumber and awakening the other half to day time activities. It deserves the title 'the greatest of the planets" as it controls and directs the activities of human and all creations. Darkness was permeating by and by slowly and quickly. Without fluttering or battering of her eyes but with the pounding of her heart my mother was stiff sitting gazing at the road to see me coming back but in vain. By 9 pm she started weeping and sobbing. I lacked commonsense to feel her pangs. Seeing her my dad too realized the seriousness of the situation. He too got panic told all the neighbours that his son fled from home that very evening. He drove to the nearby bus stations and informed the police to hunt for him but for no positive results. You can imagine the chaotic situation my mother made. She was yelling at her husband and warned and threatened him that she would leave him forever with her younger kids. Stephen Lucas was tongue tied and miserable. He took the torch and went to the cowshed and from there to the terrace of the house which was quite a large one with four divergences. Below the main terrace and the slops was the roof above the car porch. Unaware of the turbulence I caused, my dad found me sleeping on that rough floor. Seeing me he shrieked uttering- "he is here, no worries please."

"It was 3 am. Thus I was lost and found and had a good ending. All the faces including mine were serene. My mother, Lucy Lucas was the happiest. She asked me half joyously and half angrily- why did you do this to me !. To which my cool answer was – "not to you at all mum, it was to my dad who was arrogant to me. Now a lesson to all".

Doctor "was it the first and last bad experiences with your dad ?."

Francis "Not at all doctor. If it were either the first or the last I wouldn't have come to you to seek your help and suggestion."

Doctor "Ok I got you. Tell me when did you start your fights with your father ?."

Francis "Don't take me wrong, you are already taking sides with him. Older people often find faults with the younger ones, it is an always prevalent partiality to put down and snub the latter. Any way as true as I exist I never started fights with my dad but he took pleasure in doing that with me. My apologies for refuting and repudiating what you said. I don't mean any disrespect to you doctor."

Doctor "That's fine, let me know when you both had disagreements, conflicts and also your corporal inflictions from him?."

CHAPTER 3

Francis "It started from the time I was in Ethiopia with my parents."

"So you were in Ethiopia Good to know."

My parents were high school teachers and were selected by a recruiting agency in the year 1994. My parents were appointed in Harar of the Hararghe zone and the capital of the Harari Region of Ethiopia. The capital of the country is Addis Ababa where we stayed for 3 days. On the fourth day we started our bus journey at 7 am to Harar and we were told that we would reach our destination by 12 pm. It was an interesting experience for us, our first visit and travel in an outlandish place. The bus was scarcely full and so we were very comfortably seated and accommodated with our luggage. All through the journey I watched the villages and the green vegetations. The vast majority of Ethiopians lived in poorly built, dilapidated and cramped houses lacked even the basic facilities such as toilets. I can say all the people in the bus were eating certain green leaves called Khat or chat. It is a herbal stimulant, typically chewed fresh. The dried leaves are sometimes used as tea. It is consumed since centuries in Ethiopia and they enjoy it in company. Women never overconsume.

Often they eat and sing Muslim religious songs. They derive dreamy tranquility and vanity of thought. It is not illegal or controlled and so publically sold.

Ethiopia is known as the Cradle of Mankind with some of the earliest ancestors found buried in the soil. Ethiopia is the Roof of Africa with its high mountains. Haile Selassie the emperor of Ethiopia was the last in the line of the Solomonic Dynasty the one began with the Queen Sheeba. It has the largest population of any land locked country in the world. Amharic is the government's official language English is spoken only by 22% of the population even row. Beautiful scenery, friendly people and diverse culture attract many experts.

On either sides of the road we could see the tiny huts forming the villages, the people working in their fields, the green growth of various corn crops of wheat, barley, maize and teff which they call mashella (a close cousin of Indian ragi). In certain places we could see coffee plantations and thickly grown sugarcane fields. Glad to say they were all alluring treats to any visitor's eyes. When we stopped for a break and breakfast I saw the black mustard plants for the first time in my life. They grew only 5 to 6 feet tall with many small branches spreading all around the plants with very tiny beans like 6 inches long and ¼ inch wide having nearly ten to twelve mustard seeds inside. It was a surprise as it quite differed from the idea we have of the mustard trees in the bible which grow near the Jordan river upto 20 feet tall and as wide as it is tall with such big branches that the birds can perch in its shade and make nests. We opened the tiny dried beans, opened and took the black mustards from inside just for the fun of it. Apart from agriculture, rearing and breeding animals was another important occupation of the people. We saw herds of cows, goats, sheep, horses and donkeys grazing in uncultivated land. Camels were also a common sight. They are used as beasts of burden, for transporting people and goods as well as for milk. Camel's meat, wool, and leather are also utilized. All that is said here is the situations more than four decades ago. Sweaters and woolen clothes were used all through the year such was the special climatic condition in many regions of Ethiopia.

It was nearing 12 O' clock and we were more than excited to reach our destination. Then to our great surprise the driver of the bus announced that all will have one hour lunch break within fifteen minutes. A teacher from Harar was sitting near my parents from Addis Ababa. They three were in good company and he was one Mr. Alemayu Araga who was explaining everything to them. Until the driver announced the lunch break we had no concern, question or doubt about 'time'. My dad asked Mr. Alamayu "why do we stop for lunch now? It is almost time for us to reach Harar?" Mr. Alamayu, "no, no. we will have six more hours to reach Harar."

Dad, "Sir, it is going to be 12.00. The agent who made us board the bus specifically said that we will reach Harar at 12."

Mr. Alamayu Araga, "Sorry, it was a wrong communication by that gentleman to you a foreigner and newcomer to this country. Ethiopeans use a 12 hour clock with one cycle of 1 to 12 from dawn to dark and the other cycle from dark to dawn. Most countries start the day at midnight and that is the time clock prevalent internationally. Here the 1st hour of the day starts with the sunrise, corresponds to 7 am (international time) and subsequently hour by hour. The 3rd hour of the day corresponds to your 9 am and the 6th hour corresponds to 12 noon. Don't feel strange, Alamayu said, this is the biblical time too. So now it is only 6 o' clock. So the meals station arrived. My parents, siblings and I ordered only sandwich and coke. Injera is a traditional ethnic staple food of Ethiopia. Teff the grain native of Ethiopia is mixed with barley(both in powder form) is used to make injera. It is a very large thin brown or white pancake like food eaten with chicken curry which is called doro wat, a very spicy one. It was from Mr. Alamayu that we got the idea how it is made. The teff and barely powder is mixed with yeast and water and kept for three days to ferment, in a warm dark place. Eating together is an essential part of Ethiopian culture and feeding each other is often done. This practice is a bit of a culture shock for westerners and many easterners. Though teff is the main flour in injera, wheat, millet, corn or rice flour is also added as an ingredient. The injera eaten expands to three times when it gets to your stomach. While we were having lunch we saw our co-travellers sitting four or five in groups around a table and eating from the same dish. The serving platter and utential for a meal are one and the same usually. Ethiopian food is notorious by spicy, a mixture of spices of chilli powder, basil and ginger and garlic. If injera is eaten without any accompaniment it tastes tangy, bitter and sour due to the fermentation process. After the lunch and lunch break all got into the bus to their respective seats. Every one with the exception of our family had chat (Khat) with them and were chewing, singing, clapping hands and enjoying to their hearts content some even falling into naps. The corn fields were so wide spread that our eyes could not reach the other end. Luckily for us four or five fox like or jackal like or dog like animals hopped and sprang among the grown tall crops. We could not see them clearly as they were far away and pacing speedily, "which animals are they?" I shouted and pointed them out to my family members.

The answer came from Mr. Alamayu.

"They are the spotted hyenas of Harar. They are found in all habitats, including savannas, greenlands, woodlands, forest edges, subdeserts and even mountains.

Have you never seen hyena in your country?"

I answered, "no never, Sir".

Alamayu, "I will tell you something all about hyena that I know of. Striped hyenas are often referred to in literature as cruel and stupid. Spotted hyenas are famed scavengers and often dine on the leftovers of other predators. They are skilled hunters too. Hyenas have an average life span of 12 years, but can live upto 25 years. Spotted hyenas have been present in the walled Ethiopean city of Harar for at least 500 years. They sanitize the city by feeding on its organic refuse. The city's residents feed the hyenas porridge mixed with butter and mutton to mark the birth of prophet Mohammed. Spotted hyenas are easily tamed. Female ones tend to be larger than the males as well as much more aggressive. Their societies are matriarchal, even the baby girl cubs rule over the boys. It is a very vocal species, the characteristic "whoop whoop" howl can be heard throughout the night. It is also known as laughing hyena as they make giggle like sounds in times of threats and attacks. They greet each other by sniffing and licking each other's genitals, placing these dedicate organs in close proximity to an arsenal of dangerously sharp teeth. They live together in large groups called clans led by females. Striped hyenas are a bit smaller than spotted and brown categories. They have broad heads with dark eyes, thick muzzle and large pointed ears, having black stripes or their golden yellow, brown or grey coat. Striped hyenas were tamed for use in hunting. They consume the unwanted human refuse and garbage and benefit humans.

Hyenas are similar to dogs actually more related to cats. They have excellent night vision and so hunt at nights and sleep during daytime. The most striking feature is the legs: the front legs are much longer than the hind legs. This gives them their distinctive walk, making them seem like they are always limping uphill. They are agile and can run, trot and walk with ease. Hyenas are believed to be bisexual and became male and female in alternative years. Clownfish, moray eels, gobies and so on are known to change sex, including reproductive functions. It is said that the frogs can change sex during their tadpole phase. Both female and male hyenas have testes and a penis. Female hyenas urinate, mate and even give birth through appendage.

Brown hyenas are distinguished from other species by their long shaggy dark brown coat pointed ears and short tail. The brown hyena and aardwolf are not known to prey on humans. Brown hyena is well known to its weird howl sounding like a hysterical human laugh. They are solitary animals and currently the rarest species of hyena. Their speed is up to 50 miles per hour. They do not hunt in groups. They demarcate their territories by disposing of secretions that come from their anal gland onto the grass stalks. They inhabit desert areas, semi dessert and open woodland, savannahs. It does not require frequent drinking of water.They are primarily scavengers whose diet consists of carcasses killed by larger predators. Predators of hyenas include lions, leopards and crocodiles. Hyenas are fierce looking with their terrifying and seary looking teeth. The aardwolf is also called 'termite- eating hyenas and civet hyena' due to its habit of secreting substances from its anal gland. Unlike other 3 hyenas aardwolf is primarily insectivorous. Aardwolf's life span ranges from 8 to 10 years in the wild but they live upto 15 years in capacity. It is characterized by a dog like appearance. It is basically a shy animal. It has a long snout, extensible tongue, powerful claws, large ears and heavy tail and feeds especially on ants and termites. They scare away other animals by raising their long manes which make them look much larger than they actually are. It makes only soft growls and grants"

From Mr. Alamayu we heard and learnt all this. We reached the evening tea break station. We all had refreshments in a good restaurant.

CHAPTER 4

As the driver needed some rest we had a halt for half an hour. We could see the plantation of Eucalyptus trees all around that particular restaurant. We went around a bit and saw these trees growing in large numbers.

Alamayu was with us. Being a teacher in Harar, Ethiopia he was quite resourceful to enrich us with his knowledge of his country. From him we came to know many things about the Eucalyptus plantation. Its wood is used for firewood and construction. Its multi-hued bark is the most distinctive feature. A minty, pine scent with a touch of honey was felt by us as we walked about. As we continued the journey Mr. Alamayu too continued with narration of the Eucalyptus cultivation and its benefits.

"It is a medicinal herbal crop and the leaves and oil are used for making medicine. The traditional hardwoods take 118-25 years to reach maturity. They survive to 250 years in the wild. These species include grandis, saligna, globules and regnans. They grow in thick groves, the high intensity cause the falling level of the ground water table and result in the scarcity of water. The rainbow eucalyptus is tall and very beautiful with its multi-hued bark. The leaves help decrease pain promote relaxation, relieve cold symptoms, sooth irritated skins, freshen breath and repel insects. 300 to 800 trees can be planted in an acre depending on access to water, nutrients, sunlight and so on. Branch drop in eucalyptus is one means the trees use to prevent death in times of severe lack of water. They are prone to falling as they have shallow spreading roots which cannot do a good job of steadying the tree in loose soil. It is a holy tree for the Aboriginals as it causes the negative energy disappear where the leaves are burned. It is extensively used in Australia as fuel, and the timber used in buildings and fencing. This exotic tree species were introduced by Emperor Henelik in order to alleviate the shortage of construction wood and firewood. The leaves of these tree cannot be easily decomposed and cause harm to the soil. The pollen emission from these flowers is very high causing respiratory problems to humans. The golden, yellowish, red and brown branches and the trunks are very beautiful. They provide organic mulch which prevents water loss and repel insects. They are planted as the main tree species in Ethiopia. They grow in India, Brazil, Portugal, Thailand, Greece, Peru, Italy and Ecuader."

By 6 pm (Ethiopian time 12) we reached Harar.

CHAPTER 5

What makes Ethiopia unique is the fact that you will find people with a variety of skin colour and physic. Nearly half of the population belongs to the orthodox church, but there is a large Muslim population. This country is inhabited by around 84 ethnic groups. A large number of children drop out as early as grade two and only 50 percent of pupils remained in school until grade eight in 2018. So you can imagine and guess the system of education in 1994 to 1997 when I was about 12 years. Only 0.22% of Ethiopians speak English language. Primary education is offered free and compulsory between ages 7 and 12 and the literacy rate was 8.89% in 1994 and now it is about 52%. "Can the Ethiopian change his skin or a leopard his spots" Jeremiah 13:23. The name "Ethiopia" is mentioned in the Bible thirty seven times in the King James Version and is in many ways considered a holy place. Ethiopia is famous for being the place where the coffee bean originated. Ethiopia is considered never colonized despite Italy's occupation for some years. The Oromo, Somali and Tigrayaur make up more than three quarters of the population. Though the majority of the people are not white complexioned the features and looks are graceful and beautiful. They are described as "white black men". At one time in the fifteeth century, the Garden of Eden where Adam and Eva lived was thought by some to be in Ethiopia. Some say the Garden of Eden is somewhere in Mesopotania.

The very next day my parents were to report at the DEO's office Harar at 8 am as the offices and all working institutions start functioning at that time. They reached in time and were very soon attended to. My mother and father were given appointment orders to join the very next day in two different nearby schools. One employer from the municipality took us to a good and furnished house near to the schools. The department had done all possible facilities for our convenience. The medium of instruction in the primary section was only Amharic. So my sister and I had to adopt home study. As my little brother was only four years old he was free from the studies at home other than a little bit of reading and writing. My sister and I had to complete the syllabus of grade 2 and 5 respectively. After the school working hours my mum would teach us the regular academic portions of English, Hindi, Social Studies and Science and dad was helping with Maths. His teaching and my studies laid the foundation of our bad and intolerable father and son relationship. There I started my pitiable and rebellious bearance with my teacher-father. As a student my father himself was a poor one, (I heard from his father and neighbor) yet he became a teacher and a govt. employee. He expected me to understand, study very well and to be excellent. When my performance was erratic he became wild and cruel to me. I find no reason to exercise his arrogance to me. He would get up from his chair, take the palm of my hand in his and beat it against the table. He would place the outside of my palm against the table and dash my fingers against the table. Even now I feel the pain and the burning sensation. I was feeling each time he did it. With sobs, cries and rolling tears I would listen again to his teaching which I could not grasp or even listen. My mother was teaching me patiently and I could understand and cooperate. To this day I owe my English language efficiency to her and I acknowledge that to her often by saying it. When I made mistakes in calculation, addition, subtraction, multiplication and division he used to hit me and slap me on my face or any part of my body. So I wished for his absence from home.

If not for all this, I had a good time in Ethiopia. In front of our house there was a clump of Eucalyptus trees where we three used to play about along with the poor neighbouring kids who were not school going ones. Beyond the trees there was a wide and long mud hill and mud valley where we played about. On the other side of our house there was a large maize field. Actually in that day (1994-1997) no one owned land. Families made houses anywhere they liked provided it was unoccupied. Almost 90% of the houses were huts. The dwellers of huts fenced the surrounding places and considered them theirs and cultivated short yielding crops like maize, beans or other things. All the land was owned by the government. The short yielding crops including wheat and barley or teff were taken and used (eaten or sold) by the cultivators of the land. The majority were suffering from hunger and starvation. Despite their sad circumstances and situations the Ethiopians enjoy having merriment, fun and entertainment. They dance, make body movements in groups at home and restaurants during functions, celebrations and even on casual occasions. Other than the traditional dressing they also wear trousers, skirts and gowns. They never bother for daily bath, may be due to scarcity of water. Movie theaters are full on Saturdays and Sundays. We too watched movies in the theatre on every week. Two movies are displayed each time. One is always Indian movie (Hindi) and the second will be English or Chinese, no Ethiopian movie at all in those days. They loved Indian movies the best.

Dire Dawa one of the two chartered cities in Ethiopia (the other being Addis Ababa the capital) is fifty two kilometers from Harar and it took us one hour by car to reach there, the place where we liked to visit often. Dire Dawa looks strikingly different from the rest of Ethiopia, the city known for its ornate squares and strong cultural diversity. The city has railway workshops, textile and cement factories and coffee and meat canning plants and trades in coffee and hides. It has numerous culturous heritages that attract tourists. We used to go to Dire Dawa every month. As the supermarket there was an open elaborate area with many tents for different items and provisions cheaper than in anyother market place, we were frequent visitors and buyers there. One can spend any number of hours there shopping and window shopping. You get almost anything there. All the articles got there are excellent. The market is named and said as Taiwan Market. All the items there are from Japan and Taiwan. The trousers, shirts, tee shirts, saries, gowns, skirts and dresses are all from Japan. The crockerys, shoes, slippers, radios, cloths, suitcases, boxes and all fancy articles of jewellery, perfumes and colognes are all Taiwan made. Dire Dawa was a place of enjoyment for me and my siblings. We met many Indians there who owned shops of provisions, restaurants and tailoring shops. Their ancestors had inhabited and settled there. In Ethiopia there were Indian schools too Hindi being the medium of instruction. Over 2000 Indians live in Ethiopia now. From different states many come to Dire Dawa market to buy things as this being the best shopping centre in the country. Visits and shopping and window shopping were all very pleasant experiences. On some occasions my parents' teacher friends and a few of our neighbours invited us for meals at their homes. Their cuisine consists of vegetables, very spicy meat dishes in the form of chicken curry named as doro wat, thick stew and injera. Pulses such as lentils or chickpeas, beans or corn are also served. A raw meat dish of beef and goat meat with a knife will be kept along with the other dishes at the dining table. Each member at the table can cut and take the meat, dip it in the hot chilly paste and eat. Even in the butcher shop chopped raw meat is offered to those who want to eat there along with the chilly paste or powder. In the restaurants too raw meat dish is served as delicious and expensive item. It was decided that my sister and I had to return to Kerala, our state in India as we could not go on with schooling in Ethiopia. In order not to miss one year of our school year we were studying all the subjects of that year's portion:- English, Malayalam, Hindi, Maths, Science and Social Studies. As my dad was teaching me Maths in accompaniment of scolding, yelling, rebuking and severe corporal punishments I developed an avertion to studies altogether. So my father became more severe and strict with me and that in turn averted me from studies. His rage and my rebellion, our repeated and spontaneous actions and reactions ran on making me sad, worried and irritated but he was cool and unconcerned. My mother's anguish and my ails were escalating since those days. I did not want to leave my mum and little brother after a few months but I was passified by the thoughts that I could be free from my father's tyranny. The word tyranny was not too exaggerated as I was that miserable. I was 10 and my sister 7 when we left our parents in 1985. It was arranged that my dad's sister would put both of us is a boarding school and our responsibility was entrusted to her. Nothing of that plan came off. The family of my dad took it as a prestige issue. So the kids who were to be in the boarding school as the parents planned were taken to father's house where everything was under control of my father's stepmother. My mother was very upset about our not staying in a boarding school. Any way my sister and I had a bad time of two long years. The influence of our stay there reflected in both our behavior. That is all another story which doesnot fit in here. Our parents and brother returned after their contract was done with. Very soon my mum noticed that we both had some odd behavior: I would awkwardly twist my mouth and lips side to side while talking or listening being unaware of my actions and my sister was not feeling free even to talk or converse with mum. She was moody and quiet. My mum did not say anything to both of us but was vigilantly rectifying us casually. Within two months she succeeded in setting us right. I am sure we both would have been defective all our life if not for her apt interference. Any way the step mother had such influence and domination that everyone would do things which would please her. We felt out of place in that house such were the treatments and dealings we dealt with. We were offended and insulted and teased always. My sister was sad as many of her fancy things, dresses, clothes were taken away from her. It is said that the luckiest thing that can happen to one is to have a happy childhood. My childhood's unhappy things started when I was below ten with my father and it was even more felt with my father's side relatives. Then it continued without any break upto my marriage and to be frank even to this day as the recollection of my experiences flash into my memory.

CHAPTER 6

It is a puzzle to me why I remained with my family after all my ails and anguishes. I am sure that anybody else would have had quit home and find any kind of living in a railway station, bus station, or a restaurant doing any odd job. Good that I didn't become a vagabond. It is noteworthy that despite his peculiar treatment to me he was ready to send me to any college, institution or university in or outside the state to give me any education. I am obliged to him for that. I was very particular that I should become a nurse and that was granted and so now I am capable and qualified to get a job anywhere in the world.

On a 2nd Saturday my parents were off from their school work. I never liked second Saturdays as my father would be home. On usual Saturdays my siblings and I used to play around our compound or land or in the neighbouring uncultivated field under the domain of the local panchayath (village head office). This particular Saturday as usual my dad and I milked the cows, ordinary village cows yielding may be two liters milk each. On holidays (Saturdays and Sundays) happily I would take the cattle to the riverbank of Periyar, they would swim the river to reach the forest on the opposite side and I would return. After the breakfast my father allotted me five mathematical problems to be solved. I was not in a mood for studies that being a Saturday. I could not make my mind even to read the problems my father put in my notebook. I was so irritated and aggravated that I took my pen and started scribbling and scratching on the notebook page almost tearing the page with the tip of the pen. I really don't know for how long I kept on doing it. I came to awareness when my dad entered the room to check on me. Seeing what I was doing he raised his voice and shouted. The slaps that banged on my cheeks, my loud cries and his shrieks brought my mother from the kitchen to my room followed by my sister and brother. I still call to my mind that I was a boy not a teenager. He asked me to remove my boy shorts that I was bearing, I had no other go, he himself unbuttoned my shirt and I was bare-bodied if not for my panties. He took the belt and started thrashing me from my neck to feet all over. My mother was crying and yelling at her husband who pushed her away when she came in between us. The prints of the throbbing belt became conspicuous then and there and my mother pointed out to him. Somehow he was well satisfied and left the   room. My mother treated and soothed my body with hotwater, detol and balm. After that I threw myself on the bed and wept. My siblings came to me and solaced me with loving and comforting words. I was irritated and showered my angry words to them. I was exhausted and fell asleep in no time. It was on 15th May 2021, a drunkard father inflicting corporal punishments on his son telecasted in Asianet TV. The mother of the whipped autistic boy herself took the pictures of her husband's heartless mistreatment of her son and published in the mass media which resulted in the punishment of the brutal father.

From the time I saw this scene in the TV I forced myself believe.

"I am not the only one maltreated and whisked."

Yet another thinking!!!

"Why my mother who was upset and pained did nothing to save me? Why didn't she file a petition on my behalf or a charge against her husband for his cruelties to me." How could she share the same bedroom with such a cruel man."

I recollect the past incident and perceive that my questions and doubts are irrelevant and inappropriate. After bearing with and withstanding a few more episodes she had made some serious attempts and efforts she could to put an end to all these chaotic repetitions. She somehow thought that in her absence her husband would become a normal man. Twice she left the home in the morning, went about searching for a house for rent but returned doing nothing. On another occasion she went to her parents but returned doing nothing. Yet another time she sent me to her parents for some weeks when the school closed for annual vocation. Again she tried to go to Saudi to work in Varkey group of schools. On another occasion she made all arrangements to go to Anandapur in Andhra Pradesh to work as a teacher. Her plan was to take the two young ones with her. May be my mum had no confidence in my subservience as I was turning rebellious and disobedient or because she thought that leaving my dad and me to each other would reform the two of us. Even that didn't take place. I know the answer for all that nonoccurrence.

1. She didn't really want to leave me for an experiment

2. She was worried and upset at the thought about the future of her three kids.

3. Leaving the government job to purse a private job would create many future monetary problems as how she could support and provide all the needs and requirements. On the whole she could not make up her mind. Dilemma and confusion overruled her decisions.

On another occasion my mother asked me to go to the provision store to buy parboiled rice. I was more than happy as I could be away from home having some time away from my father whose presence I hated and feared. He would always be inside the house or about the house compound. Quite unlike any man of his age he would stick to the house when he had not to go to work. That made me out of place in my house. He was not a wanted or desired friend or neighbor to anybody as far as I understood.

I went to the pantry and took the parboiled rice's sack. Some quantity of the item was left over in the sack. I asked my sister who was standing by to help me to empty the rice in the sack to a container. She was about to help me when Mr. Stephen Lucas sprang up to the spot and uttered:-

"Francis, you need help for this? Learn to do things by yourself."

"Dad, let me ask you; can you do this alone without dropping the rice to the floor when you shift the stuff from the sack in to the container?."

Mr. Stephen slapped me three times on my cheek saying:-

"You start giving back answers and arguing!", Francis "I was just telling you the right thing." He slapped me again and I left the room and ran out as he was following me. He could not pace with me so he took a stone and threw it at me but I escaped it with my overspeed. Thus I outdid him and he was blown up. I returned after ten minutes, took the sack, went to the provision shop, bought the   stuff and returned home. After keeping it in the kitchen I handed over the remaining money to my mum Dad, "So finally you made up your mind." I just walked away, went to my room and lay down on my bed. Mr. Stephen Lucas rushed to my room, snatched my hand, pulled it and I was seated on the bed and was battened on my cheeks. I didn't feel any pain nor did I cry. I got to my feet as he moved a bit back. I, "After all you stoned me as if to a dog". Mr. Stephen, "After all that you did, now you complain?. Yes I feed two dogs in the kennel outside and one inside". Saying this he slammed my bedroom door and latched it from out. I didn't give up and latched it from inside. My mother Lucy Lucas, "Stephen, you do criminal abuses beating and slapping our son for nothing at all and now locking him inside the room. I am serious unlatch the door.

Stephen, "let him do it first, then I will"

My mum knocked the door and asked me to unlatch.

I said "can you make sure he won't whip me again?"

Lucy looked at her husband and he signaled "No"

Mum "Son, you do as I said, it will be OK"

Both obeyed Lucy and everything became normal.

CHAPTER 7

I was somewhat alright, I got up after a good sleep and as usual went with Mr. Stephen Lucas to the cowshed to milk the cows. I like to say about him using his name other than my dad or father as I was creating in my heart hate and hatred towards him. While I was milking, the cow kicked me and I was annoyed. I thought:-

"I can not beat back my father, so let me do it to this beast." I grabbed the cane from where it was kept and whipped the cow on its side and after that went on with milking. Mr. Stephen Lucas got up, took some cowdung in his hand and painted my cheek. Though I was disgusted and irritated without any reaction I continued with what I was doing as I was scared of that guy in that place without anybody else's presence there, though anybody's presence did not bother him. I placed the can of milk in the kitchen and my mother saw my face and told her the whole story. Despite my applying soap many times I felt that I was stinking cowdung. When I finished my bath, I saw him sitting cool and reading the newspaper. My mother went near him, drawing the chair near to him and sat beside him. He didn't even look at her. She snatched the paper from him, he in turn looked at her and made a fake smile and laugh both in one. Whatever he meant by that vehemence she was sad and sordid in her looks and expression. She said in loud voice as she had never done so far and my siblings and I heard it.

"You Stephen, are you a father? Who is Francis to you? What is your relation with him? Suppose you were a stepfather to him, I would have left you already for all that you did to him. I am bearing this only because you are his father. You should stop illtreating him right from now". Now she turned to me and said in a milder mood and tone.

"And you my son, this is all too much. Whatever be the reason behind I will leave you and your dad forever. I think that is the only solution for this." Neither the offender nor the offened uttered a word. The younger ones stood like moving dolls. The offender was cool as ever but the offended seemed released and soothed. The mediator expressed a feel of confidence, comfort and credence. Little did she know of both our stubbornness, false prestige and egoism. Thinking that her husband would be pleased she told me.

"Now Francis, the terminal exam is fast approaching. After the breakfast and some leisure time with your brother and sister make sure you sit and study English one lesson and one chapter from social science. I will give you a small test. That will be enough for today."

Francis "I will do that for sure."

As we were all having breakfast Mr. Stephen told me, "Francis, you do one thing for me too. Adding to English and Social Science, do some justice to me and Maths too. Do ten problems from Chapter 5 before evening ok?."

Francis "Ok dad done." Though Stephen sounded commanding I was positive and cool.

After the breakfast we three were engaged in playing the game of spinning tops. Mostly my brother won sometimes my sister and I a very few times. We had a time to our heart's content. I told my siblings "I am going to finish up with the study work allotted by our mother and father. After that we will again continue with our game and have fun". Within two hours I was done with everything asked and required of me. Neither mum nor dad checked the work I did. We all were happy and watched a movie in the TV at 8 pm. The movie was over by 10.30 pm and all got ready to go to sleep.

Mr. Stephen, "Francis, you go and have your bath before you go to bed."

I "Dad, I had my bath in the morning."

Dad, "That was in the morning. I am telling you to have it now. Understand?."

The reply, "I understood but I am not going to, as I said I had it already."

None of us knew what he was upto when he got up and went to the open space beyond the kitchen. Everyone was stunned by his quick move and stood stand still. He returned in the wink of an eye holding a thick, fat long cane meant to kill any snake if seen near the house premises. I had sensed his motive roughly when he left the room and was prepared and ready to go out of the room. I was already near the door to the sitout. Stephen, "Francis, don't try to fool me. It is as simple as having a bath. If you don't obey me I will not let you sleep in my house. Heard me?."

I said, "I had my bath in the morning. Now I will not have it again at this part of night". He was coming to me now and so I took to my heels to the yard lest he would have battered me. Mr. Stephen sat on a chair with the cane. Now I was standing in the car porch and from there I could see him. I moved a little distance and came with a bigger cane than his and stood near the entrance door. Mrs. Lucy Lucas, "my dear son throw away that stick. Do it for my sake". I, "Are you sure he won't beat me?." Are you able enough to protect me from his beating?. If I throw away my stick, I am sure he will whip me. My stick is for my protection, I will either beat his stick or sway mine to avoid his cane."

Lucy, "Stephen, please put back your cane. Let him come inside."

Stephen, "Ok let your son throw away the stick and I will put back mine". She pleaded me again and I obeyed and her husband too did as she asked. I felt guilty for taking the stick even with the purpose of protecting. So I decided to take bath and go to sleep. I came half the way to the room and told my dad, "Ok dad, I will have my bath and sorry for my misconduct". I was heading towards the bathroom and then Stephen:

"Now you cannot have bath in the bathing room inside. You should go to the yard, draw water from the well and have bath."

I, "why should I have bath outside, drawing water from the well when we have not one, three bathrooms inside the house?. It is now 11.30 pm. How inhuman you are!. I will take bath only inside." Stephen, "Yes, I am. If you are obstinate and mulish I won't let you sleep in the bedroom."

I, "Then where will I sleep? You are a unique father."

Mum, "No use arguing. Let's do what we can. You follow me son, I will solve the problem." She took a raincoat, spread it on kitchen floor, put a bed sheet over it and asked me to lie down and sleep on it and I did. I got up soon, opened the windows and latched the door for fear of Stephen attacking me and slept peacefully. I heard my mother telling her husband:

"If there is God you will be punished take my warning words. Do you know why I am still with you? He is your son, your blood. Just suppose, I had brought Francis as my own and mine alone son born to me from any other man, I wouldn't tolerate your brutality to him. I am here with you because Francis is yours and mine in equal share. I think I told you this already."

I was in 9th standard. That particular Saturday evening a good movie was in the TV and I told my mum that I would watch it as my annual examination was over. Mr. Stephen also knew that my exam was over. Just five minutes before the movie started I switched on the TV.

Soon Stephen interfered and said,

"Turn off the TV. Your brother and sister are preparing for the exam."

I kept the TV in mute but even then my boss was not satisfied. He said, I say turn it off !".

I, "dad, I am just watching the movements and seeing the figures and enjoying the story in the movie. In no way it hinders their studies, they are studying in their rooms. They are in no way affected or disturbed".

Stephen, "You don't have to teach me. You got to obey me blindly. Got it?"

He came took the remote and turned off the TV. I was upset, got up from the sofa and turned on the TV without the remote. He turned it off, I turned it on and both he and I kept on doing the same. My mother who was watching this silly game entered the scene, snatched the remote and turned on the TV saying, "I am not bothered about any of your interest and disinterest, like or dislike. I want to watch the movie."

She sat on the sofa watching the TV and I stood in the corner watching the same. Now the game took another turn from my role to hers. Stephen grabbed the remote and made the TV still, saying.

"Lucy, you are doing this to take sides with him against me to be in his favour. Don't try to make a fool of me."

Lucy, "Stephen don't treat me as you treat your son. You should respect my interest and likes. I want to watch the movie. Give me the remote." He did not give ear to her and she had no other go.

It was summer vacation two months of carefree time from studies. But it was not going to be a happy and pleasant time as Mr. Stephen would be enraging and torturing me physically and mentally. During usual days he would afflict torments, I would cry and weep and he would buy bakery items to sooth me on his return from work to compensate the previous day's or that morning's cruelty. I used to make cheesy jokes, while eating what he bought saying.

"I don't mind your whips if you buy better stuff to tally with your treatment to me." Scornful smiles and fake and teasing forced laughter arose from everyone at the table and even Lucy's husband joined others with an expression of uneasiness. I was always scared of my father's presence. My brother and sister were turning scared of my presence in the absence of dad and mum. I had finished with my exams before my siblings. My parents had gone to school. My sister had her exam in the morning session after which she reached home by 1 pm. She took her lunch in the plate, sat at the table and was ready to eat. I asked her to bring the question paper. She gave me and sat to eat and then. I told her,

"Wait Elsa, come here, I will ask the questions in this question paper and you answer". My sister was ok as she knew all the answers correctly. Elsa co-operated with me for half an hour, then she told me to stop as she was hungry and I would not let her. She started crying and pleaded me to let her have her lunch but I was very keen that she should obey me. So I went on asking questions printed in the question paper. She was crying and answering. I was angry as she was crying.

I, "stop crying and answer the questions". Elsa, "brother my dear, I am hungry. Let me go. I will answer all the rest once I finish my lunch".

I, "No I say"

Till now the little brother was simply watching what was going on. Now he, Joe came to the scene and asked:

"Why are you so insistent? Let her have her lunch. Why are you so rude to her?" I, "Rude to her? Ok Elsa, you go and eat. Your soliciter demands."

I dragged him outside the house to the yard. From a bush beyond the yard fense I broke and took a long and strong twig and started beating him, I don't know how many times. Joe was wearing boyshorts and the scars and prints of the stick popped up his legs to thighs. He was crying badly. Elsa lost her appetite and was helplessly sighing with tears down her cheeks. I felt extremely sad and worried about my bad treatment towards my sister and brother I told both of them.

" I was out of control of myself please pardon me, I will never repeat it." With sobs and sighs they looked at my face and said one after the other.

"its OK now."

Elsa had her lunch and went to sleep in her room. Though the exams were over my parents were not free from work as they both had SSLC public examination paper valuation I was happy about that, added to that his valuation centre was far and had to stay in the camp but my mother's valuation centre was in short distance and she could reach home in the late evenings and go early in the mornings. Even now I don't understand why I started developing a feeling of antipathy towards her too. The way I talked to her or dealt with her showed a type of repellence towards her. Every day after the shower we always changed our cloths Joe was below ten and very often wore boy shorts.

My mother noticed that Joe was not changing his trousers since three days. He was having only one pair of trousers and the rest were shorts. So she asked him to change and wear a fresh one. Joe said "It's ok, I like it".

He was holding his trousers tight to his waist. As she insisted he removed and wore his boy shorts in front of her and she saw all the scars on his legs. To her questions he was bound to tell all that happened. It was only then that I realised that my younger brother was trying to protect me by hiding the scars with his trousers. Lucky me my father was in the paper valuation camp. My mother took me aside and said. "Do you have any love for your father? The answer is 'no' because he beats you. Now you did the same to your younger ones. Don't you want their love?" I said, "I don't want anyone's love including yours. But I will not repeat what I did".

There was no change in my dad's treatment of me nor mine to my siblings. My mother was enduring all mishappenings in the house. On one occasion I was very badly threatening my sister and she was so nervous that she sat in the corner of the room like a frightened deer on her knees with both her hands clutching her chin and cheeks literally shivering. My mother was tidying up the yard and when she got inside the house she saw Elsa sitting in the corner stooping her head. My mother was terribly angry with me.

Lucy, "Francis, you should never punish your siblings to the extent of making them sick". I did not even look at her. So she said,

"Francis, do you hear me?."

I, "I heard you. I will never again do". I was rough in my talk to my mum. All were quiet for same time. Lucy was very upset. She called me to her side, made me sit on the bed beside her and said,

"Son you are going to be in 10th standard this coming scholastic year. You are going to get the SSLC book after one year. That result is going to be a turning point in your future. So you have to concentrate on your studies. You and your father are fighting, arguing and you are beaten almost every day. The situation in this house will be a hindrance to your studies. I have a plan for you, only if you are agreeing with me I will adopt it".

I was a bit excited and so I hurriedly talked over her talk.

"So mother, you want to put me in a hostel? No doubts- I am more than happy for that. I need peace of mind".

Lucy, "Now that you are fine with it, I will present it to your dad".

I, "I am sure he will agree as both he and I want to get rid off each other. Mum, I am overjoyed of your healthy ideas and plans. I am rebuking and saying bad words against you and your husband in my soliloquey always, always means always. I will be forced to spit them out."

Lucy, "soliloquey is fine but take care not to spit them out and that self control and mortification will be good for all, above all for you. So mind your words ok?."

I, "Hum m m"

The SSLC paper valuation was for fifteen days and it got over. My parents had free time from the school work and we three from studies. The very next day after the paper valuation all five of us were sitting in the verandah with our evening cups of tea and were chit chatting. Without dad getting noticed I signaled mum to speak about our new plan of my study arrangements from the month of June onwards. And she started;

"Stephen, as you and I know Francis is lagging behind his studies. He ought to improve his studies as now-a-days he is turning very lazy and slack. I think we must put him under the strict and rigorous discipline of priests who run boarding school". As we both had already planned the representation of this topic, no sooner did mother said this much than I talked over her. "It is not going to happen. I am already restricted and contemptuously disciplined here by you and my dad. You want to exile me?". Realizing my negative attitude I guess, without any reflection or pondering Stephen talked over my talk.

"Lucy don't heed to wayward talks. I am with you. Carry on with your plans. Any way how are you making a new atmosphere for Francis?". Seeing him positive we all were happy. I was the most thrilled one and my enthusiasm was that I could be freed from my dad's   battering and verbal abuse. My brother and sister were also overjoyed as they would be freed from my unnecessary interferences with them and corporal abuses. I could read their feelings when they expressed it through their looks. My mother's relief was equivalent to mine with the same feelings that I had. May be Mr.Stephen was too happy as he could win over my pretended dislike. Lucy, " As you all know my parents and siblings are in Kottayam District and I am thinking of going there with my Francis and findout a good school run by priests attached to which there will be a boarding accommodation. Every week end or alternate weekends as he likes can spend time with my parents or siblings and have a jolly good time. Today is Friday, the upcoming Monday Francis and I can go to Kottayam, knock at school offices and find out the best of all and fix at one".

Stephen, "Idea and the planned scheme are really good. Let's hope our son will make use of the new environment and get benefitted".

I, "Mum and dad, no worries. I will do my level best and secure good result for the SSLC examination". Now I too think like both of you that a change will do me good". On Saturday and Sunday my mother was busy making curries and some other food items for the three of them to serve them in her absence. On Monday morning both of us started our journey to Kottayam by the 6.00 am bus. My mother was familiar with the place as she had spent her days prior to her marriage there, her parents being there. The first boarding school we went was St.Albert's high school. The school office room of the Headmaster was not busy and so we were welcomed in and showed to chairs which we occupied. After the formal greetings the Headmaster, a priest prompted the talk.

"How can I help you?."

Lucy, "This is my son Francis Lucas, going to be in 10th standard and I would like to get a seat for him in this school along with hostel accommodation. Hope you will help us out father. Our house is in a village, the school is quiet far and the bus service is poor."

Father George, "Ma'm may I know some details about you? Why do you prefer this location? "What do you do for your living?." Lucy, "My mind was so much focused on my son's problem of studies, I forgot to tell you all that. I was a bit absent minded and sorry about that father."

Father George, "No problem at all. I can understand your botheration. Now carry on." Lucy, "My parents' residence and my native town and my place of residence till my marriage is Ettumanoor. I was a teacher in St. Mary's Girls HS Ettumanoor till I got PSC selection and got into the government service. My husband is also a teacher in the government school. We are settled in Kothamangalam."

Fr. George, "Teacher, your name please."

Lucy, "sorry again, I am Mrs. Lucy Lucas and his father Stephen Lucas. Anything else you would like to know father?."

Fr. George, no, no, that's enough. I can squeeze in Francis in standard X (both my mother and I looked at each other and smiled) but the hostel accommodation is not available (the smile on both our faces faded and immediately vanished.)

Lucy, "Father are you the warden of the hostel too?. If there is any chance, help him."

Fr. George, "I am not the warden, yet let me go and check with the warden Brother Paul if there is any vacant bed. Wait for me ok?."

Saying this he left us to the other adjacent building. We were on tenterhooks to know the principal would give us a positive response. Minutes crept by testing our patience. Fr. George returned and sat on his chair and looked at us.

He said, "Sorry to inform you that there is no vacancy at all. I wish I could help you. Brother Paul cannot do anything to help you as all the rooms are full and beds occupied. Why don't you try in St. Augustine's Boys' High school, Punnathura which is only five kilometers from here?."

Lucy, "OK father. You tried your best to help my son. Thanks to you father for all that you did. As you recommended let us try our luck in St. Augustin's". Saying this we left Fr. George and we were soon on the way to the next school.

As soon as we came to the road, we got the bus and in hardly half an hour we reached our destination. We were the fourth in queue to see the headmaster. As soon as our chance came we entered the Headmaster's office and occupied the chairs as we were offered. Keeping the experience with Fr. George my mother started with introducing me, herself and dad, from where we are and the rest. Soon the Headmaster, a serious looking priest said,

"Before going to all details, tell me what brought you here. How can I help you!." My mother's face soon showed a worried look and she said,

"We came for a favour from you to get a seat for my son."

The Headmaster broke in "in which standard?."

Lucy "Tenth Sir."

Headmaster with his grave looks:

"Is he a problem child? Why coming from so far?."

Lucy started stammering out her sentences. "Not at all. The only problem is that we live in a village, bus service is poor and he will have to spend time for to and for travel to school and home."

Headmaster, "Whatever, I can in no way help you as the school policy doesn't give admission in tenth grade."

So we moved out of the school office and then from the premises as quickly as we could to go to some other school.

We both had a feeling of dejection and our excitement about finding a new atmosphere for me seemed like sand castles. Yet we both wanted to try again. It was lunch time and we had it in a restaurant where from a co-diner at our table heard about a very good residential school under the name" St. Jame's Residential High School, Kadaplamattam run by Capuchin priests. With hope against hope we knocked at the principal priest's office room. Fr. Gregory with a pleasant face and friendly look said, "please come in both of you. How can I be of any help to you ma'm?." My mum narrated all her requests to the principal. He listened to everything patiently and said:

"So, Francis being the son of high school teachers you must be a good student. So you have every chance to get admission here. I will see to it that you get a seat in the boarding too."

Fr. Gregory's cordial talk and looks were so benevolent and encouraging that I remember him even to this day. He continued: "Francis's 9th standard result is still to come. You please bring his 8th standard marks secured in all three exams. I will count on that for your 10th standard seat." When he said the last sentence he looked at me. My mother cooly (a pretended one) said, "Yes, father" and we left. Father might have thought we would return with the mark list but we were sure that we wouldn't. We both were very badly disappointed and sad. I perceived that my mother was more sad than I was. She was sad for me and I for me. Two of my mother's younger sisters were living nearby this locality. They both knew how my dad and I were dealing with each other. My mother told the first one about all the experiences we went through. My mother told her sister that only the boarding accommodation was the problem in St Albert's school. She heard the whole story sympathetically but was quite indifferent to help me giving an accommodation in her house. Then by evening we went to the other aunt's house and repeated all the happenings. After listening to everything, she Mrs. Elizabeth Sebastian asked,

"What is the name of the school where you went first and would admit Francis without hostel accommodation?"

Lucy, "That was St. Alberts's H.S".

Elizabeth, "Mine is a joint family, the members are as you know my husband, our three kids, my father-in-law, mother-in -law, 3 sisters-in-law and 2 brothers-in-law. Francis can stay with us and go to St. Albert's as a day scholar." My mother and I were very happy to hear what she said.

Lucy, "Elizabeth, I really don't know how obliged I am to you. Your generosity is great. I know very well you do it for love of me. As I don't like to take advantage of you and that too you are living and staying with all your in laws, it is my duty that I pay for all Francis's expenses. I give you no choice to say "no" to me. So the next morning by 10 am we reached St. Albert's HS and met the Headmaster.

Father, "What brought you here again?."

Lucy, "We came to assure you that we are happy to accept your offer of admission in the 10th standard. Francis will be a day scholar staying with my younger sister and family."

Father George, "That's well and good. When the result is out, bring his marklist and submit the application form. Take care that the local guardian of Francis also come." Lucy with her folded hands, "OK Father, we will be back as soon as the result is out". And we were out of the school office. We were not excited or enthusiastic yet say somewhat happy and relieved. The 9th std marks! We reached home by 3 pm. All three my father and siblings rushed to the sit out to hear us. So we all sat together.

Lucy started, "The first school we went was St. Alberts's High School, one with the hostel and run by priest.

Stephen was impatient and said:

"Lucy first of all let me know if our Francis is getting admission or not. After giving the most concerned result of your attempt, we will listen to the details."

Lucy, "The result is almost positive like. After going through all our enquires and responses Francis and I are fixing with one.

Stephen: "OK got it. Now go on."

My mother explained all the confusions, puzzles and perplexing situations we went through in different school officers with different Headmasters. All three of them listened with different expressions on the faces. My father was brooding over and finally he said: "I don't think it will work out smooth". All became a bit gloomy. Though my mother could read her husband's reasons, as she too had the same, she asked: "why not?"

Stephen, "Let us all think together. I appreciate the generous heart of Elizabeth. But will our Francis become an unwanted guest in that joint family house?. The house belongs to Elizabeth's father-in-law. Has she any voice there?. How will all the members of the house deal with our son?. Will he not feel out place?. He may feel that he is nobody there. So think over and make decision. Once we take the admission in St. Albert's our son will be stuck in the school and Elizabeth's house for the ten months. If not for the situation of parent's job transfer, it is highly difficult to shift school in the middle of SSLC final year schooling. If any problem arises in Elizabeth's house what can we and Francis do?." If it is hostel accommodation, on the whole it is different. So take time and think over". I myself understood the practical difficulties, awkwardness and embarrassments I can be involved in. I needed no time to make up my mind in accepting what my dad said.

I, "dad, you are absolutely right. I heard you and need no second thinking, I go with you here absolutely. I prefer to bear and put up with my father's rough treatments than to be in a pickle.

Lucy "I go with both of you."

Kids, "we join you".

So everything was 'much ado about nothing'. I saw my father's guilty face when I said" "put up with my father's rough trements".

Thus that episode was over. None of the five was happy but there was no other go. All were resigned to the present situation sadly without hope for any change. Very soon everyone's premonition proved right.

CHAPTER 8

St. Joseph's Feast in the month of May was celebrated in our town with great pomp and splendor every year. People all around and even from far away crowded in the church, town and the area. My dad and his siblings, even his parents used to go for the festival every year. All the boys of my age were enjoying that feast of the church as there were countless items of entertainments. It was and is even now the festival of the town comprising all the villages and smaller towns and all the people irrespective of caste, creed, religion and haves and have-nots. Actually this festive celebrations keep going for one week and with all exuberance on the day of St. Joseph's feast and night with all animation.

For one week the celebrations were going on. On the evening of the grand function we were all having tea by 4 pm. I had already planned and made arrangements with my friends to meet together at a specific place. I was damn sure that Stephen would not permit me to go to the feast. As a precaution I had thrown my clothes through the window to the yard. In the middle of tea and talk I asked. "Dada, I would like to go to the feast celebration tonight. May I go?." The expected answer came. "No if at all you wanted you could do it in the morning and return by now. Now no."

I didn't react. As I was in my home wear clothes no one paid attention to me when I went to the yard on the side of my bedroom. Hurriedly I put on the good ones that I threw into the yard and threw the home wear inside through the window. After reaching the gate I told, "Mum, I am going for the night functions of St. Joseph's feast". All understand that I went. No one could do anything to stop me. I reached my destined location in half an hour. There were six deviated roads that led to the festivity area. All the vehicles were blocked on all six deviated roads from 1 km afar from the festivity area. As all the people were walking I too walked to the location. I was overwhelmed with all that I witnessed there. Countless people "saw I at a glance" "as far as eye could reach." The mob was pushing and carrying me, I did not even have to strain myself to walk, I was flowing and tossing among the crowd, I recall that night and I cannot explain how happy I was and I am even today. Both the sides of the lanes were lined with food stalls of eatables bewitching grownups and kids alike, resulting good benefits for sellers and satisfaction for customers. The rush and push of the mob in different parks motivated pick –pocketers who were simply profited and depressed the losers who became their victims. At different spots the various entertainer groups of musicians, band set groups, drum beaters and orchestra players camped and performed their items to their best for their own satisfaction, for applause and enjoyments of audiences and for their remuneration. I enjoyed all these concerts with my friends. Illuminations were set everywhere and the whole town was flooded with lightings. Added to that the skylight provided ample illuminations from above. Like the rooster let free in the moonlight I was blinking and walking all around in ecstasy watching this and that and everything enamoured my poor heart. But every now and then my poor mind went home and faced my enraged father. I didn't give much time to such anxieties as I was with my friends. We went to the magic show tent. The art of magic is the practice of illusory tricks to entertain other people. It is mysterious or extraordinary quality and power. The magicians use some spells and invoke the audience to see what is not real. Magic relies on powerful psychological illusions and magicians create their tricks by exploiting gaps and errors in our conscious experience. They use misdirection to manipulate what you attend to and this allows to control what you see and what you miss. The western conception of magic is rooted in the ancient Judeo-Christian and Greco-Roman heritage. It took further shape in early modern period through European exploration and colonialism after 1500. A magician is also known as enchanter/enchantress, sorcerer/sorceress, spell caster and so on. I was very happy to see the magician pulling a rabbit out of an empty top hat. That was the beginning of the show. Then he produced flowers from his hat and air. The movement of his hands were so fast that no one could follow them. His talks made the audience distract from his actions. He then amazed the onlookers with difficult tricks like cutting a lady in half and making objects disappear. Music and dances were also performed when the stage was being made ready for the each upcoming item.

After that my friends and I went to transport rides which took us from one place to the other nearby. I enjoyed that too. The balloon display was everywhere one goes and was very beautiful. To my age of that time every show was enticing. Everywhere I went I missed my siblings as I knew that they would also enjoy all this. Any way needless to say all that. We five together had enjoyed all the entertainments a few years back. There were places allotted for exhibitions. We went around and saw the fancy clothes section first. My friends bought some items of their choice. I had no money at all with me and so I felt bad in the company. So I told them:

"My father was not home when I started from home. I had only a very little balance amount from my pocket money given by my grandmother which I have already spent in the food stall." Abhilash a friend of mine:-

"Francis, no worries. I can lend you some."

I was more than happy and took the money from my friend. I went to the toy section and bought two toys: a toy doll for my sister and a ladder truck for my little brother. The money didn't suffice to buy anything for me but I was happy that I could make them happy. The next entertainer was roller coaster. Though it was much smaller to the modern roller coaster it was a wonder in my boyhood days. It is a type of amusement ride that employs a form of elevated railroad track designed with tight turns, slopes and inversions. Roller coaster was introduced in our town that year for the first time. So my family members missed it. Our next show was the famous time old story of "Allaudin and The Magic lamp" on the revolving stage. A revolving stage is a mechanically controlled platform within a theatre that can be rotated in order to speed up the changing of scenes within a show. It is a theatrical device for scene changes or shifts by which three or more settings are constructed on a turntable around a central pivot. Though a known fantastic story, on this stage it was much more interesting than reading. The formal closing of the celebration was accompanied by holy mass, benediction and a very long procession in accompaniment with band set, drum beats and orchestra and the fireworks emitting sparks and ignition. It was almost 4 am. I walked for more than half an hour to catch the bus and by dawn I reached home. My mother opened the door for me and I went to bed.

CHAPTER 9

I slept till my mother awaked me up for lunch. As soon as I awoke I asked her: "Where is my father? Is he going to beat and punish me for going to the feast celebrations ?." Mother, "I guess not. In the morning he saw large number of people grownups, kids, boys and girls and youngsters in our neighbourhood returning after the festivity. After that he told me:

"They were all talking about the exhuberance of the Roller coasters introduced this year. Our younger ones missed it. Lucy, Francis enjoyed. We all had to go, sad we didn't go. So I am sure he will not even scold you."

Hearing this I was very much relieved. When I gave my siblings the gifts I bought for them they were very happy.

Only one month was left to reopen the school. As told already ours is a remote village, even if you say it is a country side that is correct too. So it is having the facilities of a village as well as those of the country side. Though Onam is a Hindu festival everyone irrespective of religion celebrates it. So too Christmas. Every year towards the end of summer vacation our village celebrates an annual cultural programme in which competitions were conducted in all items like music, dance, recitation, monoact, mimicry, speech competition, debating competition and so on. These were conducted in the large meadow. Not only kids and youth but grownups also took part in the competitions and the winners were awarded good prizes. This celebration was an enjoyment for all agers. As this local celebration stretched to three days we three had a splendid time going and returning together. The celebration place the meadow near the village junction was very near to our house and my parents could listen the activities and the competitions from the house sitting in the varendha. I participated in English and Malayalam recitation, music, mimicry and monoact competitions and won first prizes in all that in our age group.

My sister won first prize in Malayalam recitation and a second prize in solo dance. My little brother's Malayalam recitation secured him first prize in subjunior division. The best prizes that we got are even now with our mother among her favourite collections.

Right in front of our house there was and there is still an uncultivated exceedingly large in length and width rice field with a long and shallow riverlet flowing with clear water and tiny fishes. There was a deep and round natural pool and at the pool deck there is a huge tree with its wide spreading branches and leaves giving shade all around. We three and our neighbouring friends were running, playing and enjoying our evening time there. The riverlet was right in front of our territory and we three would catch the tiny fishes using net. The water level was only upto the height of my thighs and so it was not a dangerous place to catch fish. We had rather a big fish tank erected with bricks and cement and we could make the fishes we caught grow inside the tank. They laid eggs and multiplied. Inside the tank we had lotus plants having lovely leaves and flowers. If not for my dad's peculiar nature and attitude, our house, surroundings and the land around were all really enticing to make one happy. My infancy was a very good one though I remember only a handful of incidents faintly. I was given good and nutrious food. I had all kinds of toys, toy vehicles and very good clothes. We used to go for outings. My siblings and I had the feeling that we could get anything we wanted. Until I was ten years old I stood first in my class every year. It was when we were in Ethiopia that my relation and love with my father started a reverse turn. All through his life he was ready and willing to spend money for the education of his children. If that responsibility was the criteria of love he had it. When I left him after marriage Stephen started ill-treating my brother though not so often or so rigorous as to me. So even now I doubt whether he loved his kids or his wife. He was generous enough to share his wealth with his kids.

After the summer vacation we were getting ready for school. We five together went for shopping to buy the school uniform, clothes, text books, note books, school bags and so on. We three were quite happy with the stuffs we got. Thus started the new school year. I took the resolution that I will do my best in studies for my good future and to please my mother. All the top scorers from standard IX were put in standard X A. Though I had no good scores I was put in X A by the senior teachers may be to please my parents who were allotted work in the same division of the SSLC students. My mother was to handle English and Social Science and my dad Mathematics. I didn't like to be in the classroom where my dad was handling a subject. I was bold, my father's dealings and treatments had made me daring enough to approach the Headmaster and ask him politely and gently to change my class division as I would be in an awkard and embarrassing situation in parent's class.

Headmaster: "Francis, we adopt this method of putting the children of the teachers in the class division where the same teachers handle subjects thinking of benefitting the students yet I will do anything for the good of my students but tell me why unlike the other teacher kids you prefer to be in another section?."

Francis, "I am very much obliged to you for your favourable promise but I cannot somehow tell you the reason behind my request. I am sorry about that situation of mine."

Headmaster: "OK. You can go." And I left. The Headmaster called for a short discussion with the senior members of the teaching staff who made the division sorting of the SSLC students. Among them one was a lady teacher by name Mrs. Judith Thomas who came forward with her suggestion.

"Once in the class Francis was sitting sad and distracted while I was teaching. When a written assignment was given I noticed that both the hands of Francis were marked with prints of beating with cane. I really felt pity for him. How could I ask him anything. But I could not just be indifferent. So I told Lucy teacher :{Lucy teacher, tell Stephen Sir not to beat Francis so badly}. Lucy's reply to me was that.

"Judith, Stephen is not all that he seems here. He treats Francis badly and I am really helpless. So, I think Francis wants to be in another division."

I told my mother what I did to get my division changed. She said nothing positive or negative. On school reopening day the school functioning was only upto 12 noon. That very day my parents made arrangements for tuition classes for me after the school hours every day. I was happy that I could be away from Mr. Stephen for some more hours. When I recall all my bad days and pen it down I am very very depressed. Even to this day I am not happy and I know my mother too is in the same pickle. She is not happy thinking and brooding over my position and situation now, that is much more as she attributes my unlucky experiences to my boyhood and youth. More than me she is in panic and worries about me. She told me once if she were in my shoes she would marry someone to get rid off loneliness and the onlookers' contempt as I was a divorce. To motivate she even told me that she can easily search and find a partner for herself even at the age of seventy four, if she was for it. Sometimes I feel that I should get married but at the same time I strongly feel that I am a carefree bird without shouldering any responsibility. I am unable to fix my mind, should I or shouldn't I marry.

Let me be back to my SSLC class division. I was put in X B class room and was happy about it. Monday to Friday I attended the tuition classes too. My father made it a point that he scolded me everyday for one thing or the other. Often I was beaten, I really don't know the reason. I remember only the severely bad ill treatments. One day I returned home by 5 pm bus after the school and tuition class. I had left home as usual by the 8.30 am bus. Without even changing my school wears I myself entered the kitchen and served myself with rice and curry and just started eating. Usually my mother serves food for all. Today I was so impatient that I served myself. My mother was not at all bothered about it but my father came to the dining table.

Father, "You, eating food now?. This is not lunch or dinner time. You are sitting with a full meal plate." He took my meals and threw it away with the plate to the corner of the room. Hearing the sound all the other three members came to the spot. The rice and curries were scattered in the room.

I said, "In the morning the bus was so busy, I was standing carrying my books and lunch packet, my lunch fell off my hand and a guy stepped on and stamped on my lunch packet and it got damaged. So I didn't have my lunch and am hungry. Thinking that this is my house, I took the food and without letting me talk you dashed it." I was angry but not sad. I think all had the same feeling. Though I was the victim and sufferer I felt that I won the show.

I said, "I don't want to go for the tuition. Some days I am able to reach home only after 6pm due to our poor bus service. On such days I am starving after my lunch till the evening."

Stephen, "Francis, you should not do away with tuition. As you know your tuition teacher Mr. James is a retired Headmaster, he is proficient in English, Maths and Science being a post graduate. He will guide you with SSLC question papers of the previous years."

Lucy, "Yes, Francis. The tuition will be very helpful to you with regard to your SSLC examination."

I, "I will go with both your opinion and suggestion provided you agree with one request of mine or you just leave me alone."

Mother, "We will accept your reasonable request. Spit it out."

I, "You just give me-1-rupee a day so that I can have a tea of 50 paise and a small snack of the other 50." There was a grave silence. My mother called dad to the adjacent room and after a very short time they returned and Stephen said that he would give me -1- rupee a day. The show ended.

When I was forty five my mother wrote to me in a facebook message :-

"Francis, I don't know what you are. I used to think that you became all this due to the ill treatment from your father but I start realizing that no amount of his bad treatments made you what you are now. You framed yourself by your own adamancy and cherished wickedness. You think only of your conveniences putting the lean on your father's cruelty. You really confound me. Your weepings, your flattering showered on me are all sheer cunningness. You put the blame on me when you are violent. You want to be single having full freedom. The next day you tell me that you have nobody. You are torturing me at least every fortnight. You make me sick in my old age with chest pain, numbness and confusion after your abuses to me. You do all this aware or unaware?. You are a mystery to me. Being a man of 45, make a family as you are not a strong one to live alone. You abuse me as no sons do. If I suppress or express my emotions against your verbal abuses I am repressed and oppressed by your over reaction. Come out of your sad and selfish small shell and face the realities simply aiming at your own welfare. Don't bother about anyone else. Everything is jumbled up. You yourself say you have bipolar disorder. Even your friends tell of you the same. Sometimes I too feel the same, but not sure your talks, attitudes and reactions put me in dilemma sometimes you talk as if I'm everything to you and at other times as though I am the worst. I really don't know what you are but I understand that you are full of indignation for the bad treatments received. Actually man or woman should not be alone. Each should have a life partner. It will sooth one's mind, soul, spirit and body. One feels that he/she is wanted and needed. This feeling gives importance of one's self. Feeing of self importance is inevitable for doing anything or many things important. Healthy expectations are with a handful who devote and dedicate lives with a belief in the Supernatural Being. Even here we see failures. Also King David failed. Absalom also did crimes. So I plead you to have a wife."

Let me be back to my school days. There was no change at all in both our dealings. He was turning more strict and I more rebellious and demanding. I feel damn weak, spineless and retarded while narrating all these as they are not imagination or fun but reality. My fingers and pen don't listen to the demands of my brain and they get stuck. On every Monday Stephen would give me rupees five as my pocket money for the five working days. That Monday he gave me Rs 3/- and I asked,

"Dad, why only three rupees?."

Stephen, "As you were sick last week you skipped two days' tuition classes and reached home in time. So you didn't use two rupees and I am sure you can use it for this week."

My anger knew no bounds. There was a thermos flask of coffee on the dining table which my father would take to school. I grabbed it and hurled it against the dining room wall with all my force. The flask broke with a loud shattering sound and the coffee smeared on the wall. Stephen slapped me on my cheek twice, before he could slap me again I hurled round, lifted my shoed leg and kicked the glassed shelf and a good portion of it fell to the ground with the clattering sound of the glass pieces. My father was right beside me, I don't now know whether he was ready to slap me again, I hit him on his nose bridge and he went to his bedroom. He told my mum that he had a slight bleeding from his nostrils and she passed on that message to me later. That was the first and last physical abuse I inflicted on my father and I am sure that I did him wrong. If I am not mistaken after this event we both became more friendly (not in the real sense) as he would not beat or slap me often. When I recall that day I feel guilty but at the same time I feel that, hadn't I reacted I would have had severe corporal abuses that day and Stephen would have carried on with the same treatments without any delicacy. It really taught me that rebellion, reproch and reaction will solve problems to a great extent. Even to this day I follow this, get into troubles, get tensed up. So to put in a nutshell I am where I was at the age of 16 though I am 46. Who laid the foundation for my downfall?. Who can answer? Can the readers?. Can I?. Can my mum or siblings?. Can the waves, winds, sand, clouds or stars?. Yes, only such inanimate objects can. They think not, talk not and reason not and the answer is-"Heaven knows". My mum and I pin it on him and all without any exception point fingers at me. "Judge not". How many fathers are there like Stephen?. How many mothers are there like Lucy?. How many sons like Francis Lucas?. Any way and somehow greatly noteworthy. Though my mother was an earning member like him, she never handled any money matters. She was alright with that attitude of her husband, unlike many other women.

Classes and tuitions went on, monthly tests and the two termly examinations went by and my performances and scores were very meager. Everyone at home including me had no expectation that I would get through the SSLC examination. But my mother had a dim and faint hope that I would do well enough to just go by the examination. During the whole revision and preparation holidays my mother took off from school duties to be with me at home to help me and guide me with my preparation for the public examination. She allotted me specific portions in different subjects every day of the fifteen days' revision time. I was given the previous years' question papers in every subject and without any strict interference she prompted my studies without checking my performance. On the whole she was a stimulant. For these two weeks I did justice to my studies. Even in the nights I did some hours of studies. I felt confident that I would do good in the SSLC public examination. Seeing me buried in the books and studies even my father was surprised. Days were flying and the exams started. My dad took me to school in his scooter and so the to and fro travel was easy. All the examinations were somewhat well done. I was not sure about passing the exam or failing.

Only very few families or individuals owned vehicles in Kerala some thirty years ago and my father had a scooter. The few who had vehicles let their sons of my age use it. My father would never let me and I was very angry and dissatisfied about it. One day I asked my dad:

"Dada, will you let me take our scooter just upto our little town?."

My father, "Our Scooter?. When you pay for it and buy it will be yours. You have no license. If you make an accident are you going to be responsible?."

I, "Dada, my friends who have vehicles at home use it. Why not me?. I must be able to use this like anyone else like me."

Dada, "You and I, your friends and their fathers are not one and the same."

I, "You are different from everyone else. You want to see me setting fire to your scooter and blast it if you don't let me take it now?." Dad, "Ok do it and let none of us have it." All were watching and listening us but no one uttered a word. No one knew that the vehicle's key was with me. As soon as everyone got tired of this scene and dispersed, I started the vehicle and was gone. Everyone was speechless and wonder stuck. I am sure Stephen felt crestfallen. Everybody returned to their respective tasks and interest. Very soon two working class guys came and told my dad that his son hit a working class guy and he was hurt and needed medical assistance. Immediately my father came to the spot of accident. From those who witnessed the incident my father learnt that it was none of my mistake. One gentleman told my father:

"Your son was driving in full balance like an experienced man. The guy got hit was fully drunk and was trying to cross the road in the junction. He was swaying his whole body this side and that and was pacing three steps forward and then two steps backwards. His back and forth motion would confuse any driver. If you say-'the boy hit him or did not hit him' nobody would debate. But these guys will force out help from you. Be sure, none of the driver's fault. But you have to please and passify the accuser". My father started to talk to the accuser.

"You want me to take you to the hospital to consult a doctor?."

The claimant: "You pay me one thousand rupees. I don't need to go to hospital."

To be on the same side my dad took him to the hospital. The doctor found no injury with the accuser. But he made sure that he told the doctor of all his illness he had from years ago and got all medicines. As he insisted my dad took him four times more for checkups and gave medicines for his long prevalent diseases like blood pleasure, cholesterol and artharitis. It was with much difficulty that my father got rid off that guy. The mediatorship of the leader of the working class members was inevitable for that. Both my dad and I had very little of communication, even what we had started and ended unpleasantly. As far as possible we avoided each other but it was not practical when under the same roof. One day a friend of mine came to our house to meet me. My dad was the first one who saw him. My friend was my father's friend's son. So we all knew each other. My friend Jacob had come driving his father's bicycle. When the initial friendly talk was going on between my dad and Jacob I too entered the scene. My father related every happening in connection with the accident full of scorn for me. Jacob tried to interfere in dad's talk but he wouldn't let the latter open his mouth. So till my father finished his own narration my friend kept his lips pursed. At last he said, "My father is a real good gentle man and would never abuse me before others. I had made a severe accident with this bicycle and my father was never violent". My father pursed his mouth and Jacob left. I could not pardon my father and my rage and fury were boundless as I was condemned and humiliated in front of my friend. I grabbed a long and big cane and broke the Chandeliers and pendant lights in the hall. Even Stephen got scared. My mother and my siblings started crying loudly. The rattling sound of beating the chandeliers and lights and the shattering sound of the breaking of the glasses and my moving about breaking them scared everyone in the house. I was not feeling contrition of any kind but what Jacob told about his father and his talks of appreciation about him were resounding and ringing in my ears. I was finding fault with the Almighty for my status as Stephen's son. There was silence, great silence and pin drop silence in the house.

After long hours of silence in the house my father called us all to the sitting room. We were all seated and all looked at each other. Stephen :-

"I have heard of a very famous psychologist Dr. P.M. Mathew in Trivandrum who did his studies in Vellore who can solve personal and family problems. If you Francis, your mum and I go for a counseling to him he might help us to solve our problems. If you are willing for this I will make an appointment. My mother said, "I am more than willing and ready to do anything."

I liked the to and fro journey of twelve hours as a pastime and promptly said, "If mum is going, I will also". After three days we were travelling to the capital city. As we started in the night we could be in the doctor's office by 9am. Our token number was 7 and so we had to wait. My mother was sitting with the ladies but not far from us. There were patients to see other two doctors too:- one skin specialist and the other an orthodontist. The lady next to my mother asked her: "Who is the patient among you?."

Reply:- "My son."

The lady: "Which doctor?."

Reply, "Dr. Mathew."

The lady, "What is wrong with him?."

My mother was enraged and she said,

"Nothing wrong with him."

The lady said to her friend who was sitting near her. (hinting at my mum)

"This lady is sick, she is the patient."

The three of us smiled and smirked. Some people are unnecessarily inquisitive. They are bothered about even sheer acquaintances. May be I am wrong in judging them. They must be very happy people who have no botherations and problems. They have nothing that troubles them and so they divert their minds to others. As soon as the name-Francis was called out we three went in and were signaled to seats. As we were about to sit, my father said, "Doctor, I want to talk to you alone." So my mum and I were directed to step out. After a while my mother was called in.

The doctor, "Do you also want to talk to me alone?."

Lucy, "No doctor, not at all. I rather prefer to talk in the presence of my husband." The doctor, "That sounds wonderful, be seated ma'm." And Lucy sat and looked at the doctor and wished him 'A good morning' which was responded with a smile that was serious coupled with cordiality. My mother related all the serious insults-verbal and physical that was inflicted on her son by her husband not omitting the reactions, rebellions and violent counteractions of mine. After listening to Lucy without a pause or ponder the doctor said,

"Stephen, a father like you will have a son like Francis. He developed his attitude and rebellion for his survival in your house as you state it (as yours). Unless you change, your son can not. You have to ask for pardon from him. You were totally in the wrong. I will talk to your son and then call you both again. Then you should ask for pardon from him. Ok?. Let your son drive the vehicle."

The next was my turn and my parents sat outside.

The doctor, "Francis, what have you to say about you and your parents?."

I said, "Doctor, I'm nobody in my house. I wish I am a servant rather than a son. My father is a unique one. He is a cruel man with his brutality. I wish he treats me as he does to his cows. I hate him. I am not good either. I am rash and bad too. I really have no idea how I have to be in my house. The boys of my age drive their father's vehicles, but I am banned."

Dr. Mathew, "I understood the whole situation from your mother. I told your dad to let you use his vehicle. Don't expect much change in your father. His nature, attitude and character formation are deep-rooted and hard to change. But you are still a boy and can alter your ways as you like. So, Francis, hurry up and take courage to bring about peace and tranquility to yourself, your mum and siblings. My hope is in you, not in your dad so much. Will you do justice to my counseling and relief to your aching mother? Let me call your parents. You want to say anything else to me Francis?."

I, "Doctor, please tell my dad to be considerate to me. I reacted badly, I know. I was bad just for my protection. I always tried not to react for more than four to five times bearing him. But I learnt that he wouldn't let me alone if I don't react."

Dr. Mathew, "I will tell him my boy."

My parents were called in. As soon as they came in my father turned to me and said, "I am sorry Francis, pardon me."

I knew that he was just doing what the doctor had asked him

to. May be the counsellor too knew that. I know my dad more than anyone else and was sure that he did not mean anything by uttering those good words to me. We three and the counsellor bid farewell and we went to the hotel. As soon as we entered in Stephen said, "It was a disagree and ignominy for me. What will I say to my family members about counseling and guiding principles?."

My mother always had and even now in her old age has quick wit, sharp wit and prudent intelligence. It took no time for her to reply.

My mother, "No worries Stephen. We can unquestionably handle it."

Stephen, "So easily you said it. Tell me how."

Lucy, "Stephen and Francis, listen to me. We will tell everyone that counseling was done for each one individually and separately. The counselor has stoutly suggested and requested that even we three should not share his guiding principles, remarks and rectifications to each other. This answer will be more than enough for everyone. What do you both think about my idea?."

Francis, "Your idea is really good mum."

 Stephen, "OK. We will do that."

We had good sleep and the next morning we got into the bus to our town. By 4 pm we reached home. My father's family was only five minutes' walk from our house. My siblings and all the members of my father's family hurried to our house as they saw us reaching home. My grandfather was very concerned about me always. He asked,

"Stephen tell me what did the counseling doctor say. How did he assess you both?."

My dad, "Nothing in particular other than listening to what all I said and advising me."

My grandpa, "Francis I want to hear from you. Speak out."

I, "Grandpa, he gave me some advice."

Grandpa, "I want to hear everything that the doctor said."

My mother interfered, "Father, nobody will give you a satisfying answer. Counseling was done individually to all three of us. When the counsellor was done with us, we four were seated together and he stoutly said that none of us should share the discussion and the suggestions with anybody else including us too. Grandfather said, "That counselor is a special one. I perceive that he is very clever and outstanding." That was the end of that episode.

CHAPTER 10

Thinking that Dr. Mathew the counsellor would support him and oppose me my father had taken me to him. The result was right the opposite. Even then he never thought that he was in the wrong. Till the end he was never repentant about his talks and treatments to me. If his consciousness did not prick him what is the benefit of others (his wife, father and siblings) blaming his ways. Some feel that I had to come out of all these and become successful. I myself don't know who is responsible for what I am now. As I have heard, "Man is what he makes himself." Often I condemn myself. I am really breaking down when I recall, recollect and pen down my past, and present and of my future I know not anything. Right now I, Lucy's son is a zero. My mother is very upset about me, my life and my future. I am not sure whether I will have a life partner to be with me for all my life which would be a solace for my aged mum. Though I have many shortcomings and drawbacks I will marry only a beautiful lady. I go astray from the present narration and get jumbled up.

One day I told my dad that I would like to take the scooter and go to meet my friends in our big town some twenty kilometers from home. I took enough care that my mother too was nearby and listening me.

The answer came, "Do as the counselor said. Hereafter do everything as he advised you."

I, "Dad, good to hear that. So I am going to the town with your permission and the doctor's suggestion."

It was almost 10 am and I got ready in ten minutes. All except my father wished me a 'good time' and I was off. I was feeling proud as I passed by the little town where I had got into a trouble due to the unsteadiness of the fully drunk pedestrian. This past incident made me careful in driving. Within twenty minutes I reached my friends who were waiting for me. None of us had any plan or progarmme. We just wanted to meet in a public park and have fun. As it was the first time for me to drive our own vehicle I felt very happy. It was my friend Jacob (my dad's friend's son) who taught me driving. I returned home before lunch. My father was having a grumpy face from the time we consulted the counselor. Though he was not beating me he was always showering inhuman and irritating talks to me. Gradually I was getting fed up and I took recourse in back answering, sort of 'tit for tat'. He was ok if I was indifferent like a buffoon but I could nor be so. My mother was an exceptionally perceptive personality. She decided to get a seat for me for Intermediate (PDC) in the most renowned Autonomous University cum college in India-The Andhra Loyola College- run by Jesuits strictly for boys. She was well aware of its proficiency, excellent lecturers, capable administration and discipline. When we were in Ethiopia my mother had a teacher, co-worker and friend from Vijayawada, Andhra. Now and then they both were contacting each other. From that friend Alice Fernandez my mother managed to get the phone number of the then principal of Loyola College, Vijayawada. He was Fr. Abraham Lopez. My mother had to make so many calls to get him on the phone as he was always engaged with guardians of the parents of applicants- as it was the time of admission. As the principal was impressed by my mother he was positive about giving her son a 'seat for the two years' intermediate course. He asked her to come to the college office and meet him along with me as soon as the SSLC results were published. Though I summed up the conversation in a couple of sentences they both were talking for more than half an hour. From her response to the principal, it was clear that he collected our family background and discipline. We had to wait only for a fortnight for the SSLC result. The overall situations in our house (as Stephen asserts his house) was not good. There was not even a single day that my father did not scold me or abuse me. So we both were not loving or friendly. My mother was not happy or friendly with my dad, was not pleasant with me too but somewhat sympathetic. My siblings were not happy or friendly with me as I used to dominate and talk bad to them whenever Stephen was not in the surroundings. I used to go with my friends to play football where I made quarrels and fights and nobody liked me. I did not much bother about this as I felt that I too did not like any of my friends. Why friends?. Did I like my mum for all that she suffered and did for me?. Did I love my father for being ready to do anything for my education?. Did I love my brother and sister who were younger to me?. I somehow felt that even my mother loved them more than me. I was thinking that I will get a seat in Loyola as my mother was behind the screen. I also decided that I will make good friends and will do better studies in the new place, miles away from my father's interference.

The S.S.L.C. result was out and I passed. I have no words to say how happy and excited I was. I really don't know to explain how happy we five were as I was in the borderline. My mother's plan was to go to The Loyola College and make all arrangements with the principal for the college admission and with the warden of the hostel for my accommodation. As everything was almost prearranged with the college principal there was no worry. My mother contacted the principal on the phone and an appointment was made to meet him in person. After that she made a special lunch to celebrate my success in the SSLC examination. We were also very happy. Within one week I got my SSLC Book. I had only fifty marks extra to the mere pass. My scores in English language and social studies were the top most. Even before getting the marks my mum and I had made plans that I should opt the group of History, Political Science and Economics. Though my dad was all that I said, he was always ready to do anything for my education and good future. His dictatorial personality, attitude, behavior and actions were his only drawbacks. My father went and bought our train travel reservation tickets to Vijayawada. We were to meet the Principal on a Thursday before noon. So we started our journey on Wednesday afternoon and reached the college office by 11 am. We waited for one hour and the principal was ready for us. Our talks and discussions were friendly and pleasant. But the Principal was not pleased with my marks. After making a study of my scores in the various subjects Fr. Abraham Lopez suggested that I can be good at arts subjects. We blindly supported his idea as we had already picked the Humanities as the best for me. The principal gave the application form to be filled and signed by the applicant and co-signed by the guardian to be submitted in the college office which we did. From the office we were directed to the hostel and hostel warden- Father Charles Morris. In Fr. Charles's office too we had a talk and interview. After the conversation Fr. Charles:

"Francis, I know that you are happy about getting admission in this college. From my part I tell you to recall this day everyday and renew your happy feeling which will help you to b a good student in the college and a disciplined one in the hostel. I want you to be very good as your parents are in another state and so it will be difficult for them to come all the way here if any problem arises."

I, "Father, I will abide by all the rules and regulations of the college and the hostel." Father Charles and my mother were very happy to hear me. The principal and the hostel warden gave clear idea of the fees involved.

By the evening train we returned to our state and home. I was very happy as everything was finalized and settled. I was to reach the hostel the day before the college started functioning. I often have a feeling of inferiority when my friends talked highly of their fathers and their friendly talks with them and their loving dealings. I was always a silent listener then. But now I felt an air of importance and superiority when I told them that I joined for intermediate course in Loyola College, Vijayawada when they joined the local college in the town. Like everyone else of my age group I was excited about the fact that I was no more a school boy but a college student. I was going to be free from my father's incessant interference from my talks and doings. In my mind and thoughts I was escalating. I wanted to become a hero in the company of my friends. Whenever we met in the town one or the other used to pay the bill in the restaurant but I could never afford it. Before going for my college studies it was my wish that I gave a treat to my close friends. But how to get money. As I knew very well that my mother never handled money matters, she could be of no help to me in this respect. But I had to find a way. My father would never understand my need and my mother had no means to help me out. Very soon I hit at an idea. There was a cumbersome bundle of natural rubber sheets made out of rubber latex (sap) in the store room. I somehow managed to take six rubber sheets and packed it well. I gave them to our rubber tappers's son Jerry Mathew who was my friend and neighbor and asked him to sell it for me. That money was good enough to entertain my friends. This was my willful wrongdoing of the first time. Sad to say I was caught. My mother was always keen, observant and scrupulous. A few days after I sold the rubber sheets my mother observed that a few of the sheets were missing and she asked me about it. I could not but say the truth and pleaded her not to tell dad about it. Here she was not on my side and she let my dad know it. I was scared of a verbal and corporal punishment. He asked me how I did it and I told him that Jerry Mathew helped me.

Luckily for me, beyond my belief my dad just finished the topic asking me never to repeat. As he did not even scold me my feeling of guiltiness and remoursefulness increased. I also felt that I belittled myself before my siblings. Being the eldest I was a bad model to them.

In Kerala, my state the schools reopened in June first week as usual. My parents went to school to work and my brother and sister to school to study. As the college was to start on July first week I was at home. Here the colleges too functioned in June. So, I had no playmates too to spend time with. As far as possible brother and sister were keeping a distance from me as I used to scold, find faults and even beat them. Knowing my nature my mother had asked them to avoid me. Though I know why she did so, I hate her for that. Every evening and night my siblings were busy doing their home works and routine studies. I knew that they both were hardworking, quiet and studious and scored good marks always. I made up my mind that I would be like them and study and score good marks once I am in Loyola. Paradoxically I was not ready to start some reading in English though my parents bought and gave me some English story books to improve my English language. All that I know of my yearning of those specific days was that I wanted to go to the new place and situations, get rid off my father's unsolicited interference with everything said and done. One day my parents came home late after their work. They had done some shopping for me. I liked the suitcase they bought for my travel and hostel use and the carry on bag. All the articles needed for the daily use like paste, brush, comb, mirror and so on were also bought. Only clothes (college wears and hostel wears) shoes and slippers were left to be bought which my mother and I went after a few days and bought. Thus I was almost ready to go, but a few more days to come.

From my adolescence I am now making a long skip to my early middle age. My mother Lucy left me a message in my whats app page.

"Francis, you told me many times that your dad made you strong enough to face any difficult situation and sorrow may be you are that now. I don't know exactly your position now as you are a riddle to me and so my assessment of your personality and mentality are obscure to me your mother, so who else knows you I wonder !. You are often an impetuous and wild horse. In a moment you weep and sob, without a gap you become rash and impulsive. So where you stand, I know not. I was and I am in panic and scare. For long years I was able to face and would find some reason of justification for all your talks and behavour. But now I become numbed in head. Mind and heart are close friends. So be careful. Your forehead, temple, mind and brain are closely connected. From my own experience and endurance I understand this. I used to be scared of Stephen's and your actions and reactions every day. Now I am scared of your phone calls, voice messages and written messages which are often abusive and beyond endurance. Can I not pick your call!. Can I disconnect your call? I am lost both the ways. If you or I don't contact I am lost. What is my choice? Right now and sometimes I feel my chest is rising and falling as I breathe. May be my old age pants."

On the intended day my mother and I reached Loyola College hostel. The warden welcomed us heartily and took us to the room allotted for me. The room was quite spacious with two bed room accommodation. So the roommate was to reach before the closing of the day. Before my mother left the hostel room, she handed over to me the hostel fees for the first semester-till December. She left me saying to pay the hostel fees every month. Considering many factors she was happy to leave me in the Loyola environment considering just one factor, I was happy. After four months my mother came to the Loyola hostel. The warden sent the attendant to bring me to the hostel office. To my great surprise I saw my mother seated there. I was offered a chair and I sat. The warden started:-

"Ma'm, I sent you the message only the day before yesterday and you are here today. Could you get a train ticket reservation so soon?."

Lucy, "no father I just bought the ticket over the counter and came off. As the message said that Francis will be expelled from the hostel as the hostel fees not paid for four months, I hurried here with the money."

Warden, "But being teachers you and Francis's father didn't bother to pay the fees after July. Why?"

Lucy, "Francis was given the hostel fees for the whole of first semester. We were thinking of paying the second semester fees in January. Any way sorry Father it was not paid."

His face turned black as he looked at me. "Francis, what did you do with the four months' hostel fees?. You came so far from home to study or squander money with your friends and enjoy a jolly good time? You can have all that once you finish your studies and earn a living. Now leave aside unwanted luxuries and concentrate on your studies. I warn you in time that if you don't give due importance to studies and hostel rules and regulations you will not accomplish the aim with which you came here. Ok?

I, "Father, sorry for my irresponsibility. I will try to be what my mum and you wish from me."

Warden, "Try to keep up what you said."

I, "Ok Father."

My mother paid the whole sum of the first semester to the warden.

Warden, "Lucy teacher, hereafter please send the hostel fees of your son into the 'warden's account every month. Ok?"

Lucy, "Sure Father, as you say."

When I was with the warden I had put on a face of repentance for not paying the hostel fees. As soon as I was alone with my mother my mood and attitude changed.

I said, "You people don't give me enough pocket money. All my friends have ample money for every need. I feel ashamed that I have no money as much as my friends have. Very often the hostel mess food is horrible. Then like any other friends of mine I too go to the restaurant adjacent to the hostel gate and eat. When they supply less quantity of breakfast and evening refreshment my recourse is this restaurant. They don't give me free food. From where will I pay?. So I used up the amount you gave me for mess fees. Again, on Saturdays all the hostelites go for movies. Do you expect me to be sitting in the room? I am like anybody else. You got me?". I was so rash and furious in my voice and expression that my mother was scared to open her lips and tongue. When my mother was sighing hearing me, I really scolded her saying not to pretend. So she had to suppress her feelings and control her reaction tongue-tied. From that time onwards I kept a yoke on her neck. As I write it I'm taking deep breaths. Her return train was in the evening but she wanted to leave to the railway station. She opened her hand bag and gave me some money saying;

"You will be coming home for Christmas vacation soon and so you will be able to meet your personal expenses with this." I counted the amount and became more furious with my mum.

I, "Only this much? Where should I go to meet all my needs? You shouldn't have send me here. I would have been OK with home food."

Lucy, "I don't have any more to give you. I paid a huge amount to the warden which was pending due to your extravagance. Now let me go to the railway station. If I get seat reserved, it, will be comfortable for me as I didn't sleep last night.

I, "You are bothered about your comforts, not mine."

Lucy didn't want Francis to come to the station, but he wanted to. I knew that my mother wouldn't take a reservation ticket rather save that. She was sitting in the waiting room and I was restlessly walking back and forth on the platform. I knew that she could give me some more money but she wanted to put check on my extravagance. I became more angry and rushed to the place where she was sitting. I saw her brooding over something (I knew it was about my violent dealings towards her) and weeping. But I had no tender feetings towards her as my whole concern was to extract money from her. I banged on the table on which she was resting her elbows and yelled at her.

"Give the money which you have now with you. I don't mind stopping my studies." I stood near her, showered rude and angry words on her- all for no use. My rude and rough attacks of words on her, my aimless and to and fro walks on the platform and my mother's weeps and sighs continued till the train arrived. She got in a compartment which was almost empty. I too entered the compartment. We both had nothing to talk. My mother opened her purse and gave me all the money left in the bag.

I refused to take saying:-

"Mum, I don't want it. I will and can manage with the sum you already gave me. I am OK. Keep it with you." She was very keen that I took it and so I did it. As the train started its shoving movement I got out of the train, stood on the platform waving at her and she continued waving putting on an artificial smile. The huge long vehicle started its noise and vibration with its clickety-clack sound.

CHAPTER 11

It was a Saturday evening that Lucy reached home. Stephen and the two small ones came eagerly to listen to all that happened with Francis in the hostel. None of the four found any excuse for all that I did in the hostel or to my mother. Stephen was terribly dissatisfied on my irresponsibility and rude dealings to my mother. I knew that I was wrong but don't know why I was not feeling guilty. Though I made my mother miserable and sad I was not feeling any sympathy for her. I was only worried as to how I would get enough pocket money for the next and last term of my that scholastic year as the warden has asked to send the hostel fees to his account. I was actually not interested in studies. My only longing was to spend time happily with my friends. Christmas hols were approaching. My only aim was that I should bring money with me for the next term expenses. In my home town I had five good friends. They told me that they are making money for their personal expenses on their own. They ensured that if I joined their group work I would be benefitted. I was more than happy to join them. Their work was as follows:-

There are unlicensed money lenders. They lend money to customers without taking any surety but they extract heavy interest. Many fall in their trap and sometimes the other way round. Some people borrow from these money lenders to buy vehicles. The lenders keep with them one key of the vehicle and certain important papers. Some pay off the borrowed sum and settle matters. A few fail to do this and drop paying the amount and interest. That causes great loss to the lender. Then they employ certain seizers to seize and bring the vehicle to them, giving the key, the address and details to the seizers. The money lender would pay his appointed vehicle seizers once the vehicle is brought.

My friends were doing this work for the unlicensed money lenders and earning for their pocket money. I was keen about joining my friends and doing at least two such undertakings to get some money during my twelve days' of Christmas holidays. At the same time I had two problems. I, scared how I could handle Stephen's questions about the nonpayment of hostel fees. My mother was scared of me and so I could manage with her but he would never be scared of me. Secondly how I could go with my friends to do what I planned with my friends. The very next day I got money from home for my train ticket and reservation for my home journey. I could easily travel without a reservation and so I saved that amount for my pocket money. As I was not recognized at home I felt happy and proud that my friends regarded me as a notable one among them. I reached home on Christmas eve. The crib, the lighting and the three magi's star were all set beautifully. Lucky for me and the other members of the house that my dad did not ask or even mention about my extravagance. I felt I was blessed by the Holy family. After the midnight mass and the nativity ceremonies we reached home, cut the X'mas cake, enjoyed it and went to bed.

Our team leader for the operation of seizing the car was my best and most loved friend Peter Antony. He took a contract from Mr. Paul James having the key and essential details of a car owner thirty kilometers away from our town. He was one Mr. Davis Alex a lower division clerk in the revenue office. He was the only earning member in his family having his aged parents, wife and two school–going kids. It was highly impossible for him even to make the two ends meet. Yet he was leading rather a lavish life, having loans, yet a self-important jerk. The loan and the interest payment was due for seven months though the money lender Paul James demanded and requested to pay the pending sum. Davis Alex only made promises every month making some excuses. Mr. Paul James could not tolerate it any more. He wanted his money and had no hope that he could get it.

* * *

CHAPTER 12

On 27th I was to meet Peter Antony the coordinator of the seizing operation at the town bus station waiting room where another friend Siva Kumar Nambiar was also to join us at 8 am. From there we three were to go to the Revenue office parking lot by 9.30 am. I was already changing my principle of obedience to my parents, even then I was doubtful as to how I could represent my plan to go out and meet friends. My boldness overruled my hesitation. On that day morning we were all having our morning tea at the dining table as usual. Many have bed coffee but we had tea as Stephen and his family had the tradition of having tea which my mother too adopted. I wanted to say but reluctant, continued sipping the hot tea, yet wanted to say, again reluctant. My mind and mouth were wavering. Everyone was finishing their tea, I had finished and said:-

"Dad and mom, I was away from my friends for a long time and I want to meet them today. I am sure you understand me."

Lucy knew that I would go at any cost. So without giving a chance to Stephen to talk she said:-

"We can understand your reasonable wish to meet your friends. I'm sure your dad will also have no objection."

I said, "that is enough and more for me."

Stephen and the younger ones had disagreement on their faces, Lucy somehow put on a tolerating face and as for me an adventurous thrilling expression. Without waiting for the breakfast I was off from home. When I reached the waiting room both Peter Antony and Sivakumar were already there. We got into a bus which was going to the city of Alwaye where the Revenue office situated. It was only 9 am. Nobody would come to the office that early as the working hours started only at 10 am. So we went for breakfast in the nearby restaurant. In those days only very few owned cars and 80% of the people used only public conveyance and so there wasn't any parking lot for the Revenue office. There was only a public parking lot spacious enough for may be about thirty vehicles:- cars, bicycles and motorbikes. The number of the car to be seized was KLQ-71706, a green coloured Maruthy 800. The number, colour and the brand was printed in my mind. We three were standing at three different spots in wait for Mr. Davis Alex to come and park his Maruthy. There was a bus stop very near to the parking lot and so many were walking about hither and thither so none of us was in any way the centre of attention. Minutes were lingering and dragging by arousing my impatience. At every short intervals I was checking the time. No doubt the other two were doing the same. At each horn I would open wide my eyes in anxiety. Any way time must pass, office must function and Davis Alex must come. Putting an end to my searching looks there came the green Maruthy and the owner parked it under the shade of a spreading tree. We three could see the car from each one's location. We watched him locking the car, climbing the stairs to the office. As planned earlier after identifying the vehicle each one of us walked to the nearby park individually and sat on three different benches. There were only a few young boys like us who were sitting together and chattering. Understanding the good opportunity we three came and sat together and decided how to proceed and carry out the plan. Sivakumar and I were to walk in a little distance away from each other through the pedestrian path while our leader Peter

Antony would go to the parking lot and drive the car and pick us. So he moved towards the parking lot and we two on the road to Ernakulam where the money lender Paul James' little office was. Peter was astute and adept to use the duplicate key as if he were the owner and handled the adventure and risk as an experienced one. In a couple of minutes' gap we both were in the car. The car moved and the sighs of relief were breathed out. I was so thrilled that I could not talk anything. At the same time I was scared too. Every now and then we were looking at the rear to check if someone was following us. Luckily for us none of that happened. Peter Antony was a good and smart driver and was driving fast and safe. At fifteen minutes' drive distance from Paul James' office the car came to a halt in front of a public calling booth. We three alighted from the car, Peter entered the booth to inform the money lender that we were at hand. After that then and there we got inside and resumed our journey. My heart was pounding with all kinds of anxiety as we were nearing our destination. Any way this feeling of agitation and concern haunted me only for a few more minutes and it came to an end as our leader Peter Antony announced:-

"Friends, Francis and Siva Kumar, here we are!. Look at our boss standing eagerly to meet us."

Mr. Paul James took the key from Peter Antony and parked the car in an interior area. He did it soon and directed us to his office. We followed him, he made Siva Kumar and me sit in the sitting room and guided Peter to his personal cabin. They both had some personal talks and dealings. The boss had not made any other appointment or invited any guest or visitor for half-an-hour. Once their deal of this case was over they both came to where we two were seated. We four had coffee and snacks and we parted. He thanked both of us for our earnest co-operation in the deal. Now we three were walking to the bus station for our return trip. I was very eager to know everything especially the remuneration for the risky work done. So I asked,

"Peter, what did the boss say about the whole operation?"

Peter, "Francis, let's get seated in the bus in a comfortable and convenient zone. Don't ask anything now."

I, "Ok, I got you."

We reached the bus station and read all the boards stating the name of the place it was going. Right then a bus came and parked. The conductor put the name board and we knew that it was going to our town. The driver and the conductor got down, I went and asked the conductor its scheduled time and understood that it had a delay of thirty minutes. We happily got in and occupied the back seats. No one else was in the bus. Peter soon opened his wallet and gave Rs 1000 to Siva Kumar and me as our respective share and we were happy. Thus my first effort to get pocket money was successful. That was a good sum in those days, my hostel fees for a month was then Rs 400/- and so it was a considerable amount. The passengers started entering and occupying seats. So we changed our topic of conversation. They wanted to hear about Vijayawada, Loyola College and the hostel life there. As my friends had never gone out of state they listened to me with eagerness and interest. They felt jealous of my advantageous position as a student in Loyola. But only I knew that I was not doing justice to my opportunity other than learning to talk in English under the Jesuits and in the company of non-Malayalam speaking friends there. Siva Kumar got down from the bus as the location of his house was before the town bus stop where Peter and I wanted to get down. In ten minutes' time the bus took us to our location. Peter and I went to the restaurant and had a splendid lunch. My friend told me that we would go to the park for a short while and we went. Together we sat on a bench. I said,

"Peter I am so happy that you made me work in this deal and I am very very happy about the sum you gave."

Peter, "I want to tell you about yet another undertaking. That is the reason why I took you to this park."

I, "Peter, I am very curious my friend. Come to the point."

Peter Antony, "When Paul James finished all the procedures of the deal we three did with him said, "Right now I have one more deal. If you are ready I will hand over that too to you. What do you say?".

Peter Antony, "I will be obliged to you for that. Don't have any doubts about my willingness or readiness. I am always at your service, Sir."

Paul James, "The case is another one of the same kind. Here my borrower is one Mr. Abraham Jose who works in the Munsiff court of Trissur. I want this to be done before the New Year. Can you do it on the 30th of this month, only three days more."

Peter Antony told his boss:-

"Be sure boss my friends and I will get it done."

Then Peter to me:-

"Francis, on this deal we will take our friend Albert Sebastian. What do you think?."

I, "Peter, he will be good enough." We agreed to meet in the same park at the same time as toady on the 30th and parted. This was my first time earning and quite a good sum of Rs 1000/- That very evening when we were all sitting together and talking I told:-

"I have to go to Loyola on the 3rd of January. I want to reserve my train ticket. Again I want to meet my friends once more on the 30th as we planned and want to go for the morning show in the movie theatre."

Stephen, "Francis, even if. I say 'no' you are not going to obey me and so I have nothing to say."

We switched on to other topics as no one wanted or liked to support or oppose my plans. I was always feeling that I was an unwanted one in the family. I hated the pricky and insulting talk of my father. I was full of appreciation for my mother but I hated her too. I often flattered, even sincerely praised her but more than that I very often showered my wrathful and scornful words to her. This characteristic of mine continues even to this day. She asked me openly when I was in good moods and terms with her why I hated her. My only response was:-

"You loved only my brother and sister.

 I was nobody in the house.

You asked my siblings to keep distance from me.

You never entertained my friends at home."

Lucy, "I have my answer Francis. You threaten, pick quarrel and fight and beat and punish them for no reason at all. So I asked them to keep away. Your friends were using alcohol and were even scattering food around the plate and on the floor and your dad was offending you in the presence of your friend on another occasion. Any way we both have assessment of each other and hardly any chance to rectify as you are forty six and I seventy four. We cannot snatch or grab love. But I am a mother and you?". I was in my late teen age and as I was rebellious and disobedient my dad did not control me much. I went about with my local village friends and this was what every other boy of my age did. So I didn't feel guilty at all but I didn't like my parents' expectations of me.

As planned and decided Peter Antony, Albert Sebastian and I reached Trissur city bus station about 9.30 am on 30th December. The munsiff court was ten kilometers from the place where we were. As we didn't want to be late we took a taxi to the court office ground. The parking lot was wider than that of our first operation spot of Alwaye. We stood in wait at three different spots looking for the ivory coloured Escort car with the name plate No KLT 47000. We were stuck where we were up to 11 am. Many cars came and got parked but our Escort didn't appear. Finally Peter went to the court office, met the office attendant who was serving tea for the employees and learned that Mr. Abraham Jose was on half day leave and would be in the office only in the afternoon session. We three went to the shopping mall just for window shopping just to pass time. Before 1 pm we had our lunch and reached the operation spot and stood in our respective spots waiting for Escort. We waited only for five minutes and I saw an Escort in off white (colour) coming to the parking lot. Immediately I signaled my friends and our anxiety aroused. When we checked the number of the car our thrill went with the wind. I also noticed that the colour of the car was not ivory but off white. We stood at our places in "stand at ease" position though in dilemma. Any way Abaraham Jose had to sign up in for the afternoon session by 2pm. So I knew that our time of operation was fast approaching. To my great surprise the ivory car entered the parking lot. I looked at the number plate and it was the same. The owner cum driver parked the car in the parking lot. We three saw him entering the office of the court. All three of us had sighs of relief. There was going to be a public exhibition in the city for one month. So they were camping and putting up tents. As planned we walked to the exhibition ground. We just walked around the different stalls for half an hour and then Peter Antony walked back to the car park. The Escort car was lying in wait for Peter. Without wasting any time he walked to the car, turned the key in its door key hole, got seated in the driver's seat and slowly took the car from where it was resting. As decided already Albert Sebastian and I were walking through the foot path leading to Ernakulam route. Peter was a silent and cool snatcher and seizer of car and came with the car and perched it ahead of us. We two reached the vehicle, got in and was off. It took us two hours to reach Paul James.

Until Paul James and Peter Antony were done with their private dealings we both were stiff sitting in the waiting room. After the formal and friendly dialogue with the money lender we three hurried to the bus station. Peter Antony had shared the benefit of the successful operation 'Ivory Escort Car' with Albert and me in the waiting room of Paul James to avoid anyone's eyes. After Albert parted Peter gave me two hundred and fifty bucks more and I was much delighted. I reached home in the late evening. No one asked me anything about the reservation ticket to Vijayawada and I was saved from cooking up some false story.

CHAPTER 13

Only three more days were left for me to go. I didn't know how to be a loving son or a lovable son in the family. So too to be a loving or lovable brother. I enjoyed the company of my friends who regarded me as an equal to them. I had such friends in my home surroundings, our town and hostel. Now as a middle aged man I have no friends at all, no life partner or a family of my own. I am right now lonely and outlander where I am. Sometimes I feel that I myself am responsible for what I am now. But often I feel my home environment, my dad's cruelty and my mother's ignoration amounted to my unluck. I am like one who is chasing two rabbits at a time.

I wish to settle down in my own native land as I feel and am a foreigner here. On the other hand I see the future benefits of life in this foreign land. I am in between the ferocious devil on the shore and the deep sea. How can I save myself when I put one foot in one boat and the other in another one !. I am puzzled. All these thoughts worry me and upset me now in 2022 when Covid and its variants keep devouring lakhs of humans all over the world. Will this cruel pandemic keep on its gambling with life as long as the world lasts? New variants, new findings, new remedial measures, yet deaths, burials and cremations. Certain facts and thinkings pop up to my brain and mind and they spring forth on my writing paper through my pentips.

Now let me be back to my teens. My dad's (severe) restrictions motivated me to do things at my pleasure and my rebellions unmotivated him from doing corporal harms to me and motivated his verbal abuses to me. In both the ways I was lost at home and so my preference was to be outside of home. My friends and I went fishing in the river, boating in the river, swimming and bathing in the river. We spent time playing football, quarreling, arguing, fighting and beating and getting beaten. In those days did I love my family members or my friends more?. I really don't know. I was feeling good and energetic in my place with my village and neighbourhood friends and my companions in the town but only the interference and check by my parents. I was equally good and happy with my company in Loyola College and hostel and there my controller was the hostel warden who was checking on me all the time and bringing me to task, yet more tolerable than my parents. The day came for me to go. All four of my family came to the railway station to send me off. I was feeling sad to leave my brother and sister, a little bit to leave my mother and quite immune better to say glad to leave Stephen. My friend Abhilash Mathew who was my class mate and hostel mate reached the platform. My mother was happy that I had a friend to travel with me. It was almost time for the train to arrive. We started hearing the *choo, chung, chuff* loud and soft sounds of the approaching train –there it came and stopped and waited for ten minutes giving time for the passengers to get out and get in. After being seated I looked at my family members standing on the platform. I could see tears in my siblings' eyes and also noticed my mother with the suncken eyes. I felt that my eyes were full and my friend Abhilash teased me and I laughed. The whistle blew, the platform bell rang and gruff horn sounded. The train started its slow motion forward, soon gathering speed and in the wink of an eye it was in full speed with its trumpet sound and howling. We lost sight of the long vehicle. The hustle and bustle on the platform vanished. Abhilash was a good friend of mine but not naughty and restless like me and had good parenting unlike mine. His parents were also teachers. We both had another friend- classmate and hostelite Sebastian Thottam. His house and family was in Guntur where his father Joseph Thottam was running an English medium primary school upto 5th grade. In those days degree or teacher's training certificates were not compulsory to be a teacher. Ability to teach and the needed proficiency in English, efficiency to handle the students, knowledge got after preparation of the subject and the good impression created before the school authority would suffice to become a teacher. Even today in many states of India these criteriums are adopted in some cases. I always found pleasure and delight in train journey. The jerks, the swayings, the facility to move about, the different stops, the beautiful scenery watched through the windows and the chain of its own sounds of whistles, horns and machines and engines and all enchanted me always. When the train reached Vijayawada station Sebastian was waiting for us on the platform. On the way to the hostel Abhilash Mathew said, "I hate my life in the hostel, always obey the bells for chapel, dining room and study room. To be punctual always I restrict myself."

I said, "But I am fine with all the bells. I reach the chapel only when the mass is half over as I get up only at the bell for mass. I come to the refectory only after the food is served. To the study bell I will be the last one to enter the study hall. But to the interval and recreation bells no one can beat me."

After the college working hours followed by the 4 pm tea we were allowed to go out of the college campus on condition that we were back to enter studies at 6 pm. Towards the end of January the intermediate students were going to have a study tour to Delhi and Agra. I wanted to join the group. The warden of the hostel allowed me to make a call from his office to my home. The phone was picked by my father and cooly he agreed to send me money. Abhilash and Sebastian were also joining the excursion group and so my excitement doubled. The money

I got for joining Peter Antony for seizing the ears was good enough for my lavish expenses during the tour.

CHAPTER 14

DELHI AND AGRA

I had no interest at all in my studies. I never paid attention to the lectures in the class. My mind and thoughts were with my bodily and mental anguishes in my home. I really don't know why I hated my mother. I had no loving or tender feelings towards my siblings too. Even to this day I get ecstatic talking offensively to my mother and siblings. Even then with aching heart she talks and listeners to me where as my brother absolutely avoids me and my sister discards me often.

It was the day to start our trip. All were ready with our bags. We were one hundred and twenty nine boys and nine lecturers for the trip. It was two days' journey from Vijayawada Junction to New Delhi Junction. Our authorities had made all convenient arrangements. We had taken two compartments for us. So our journey was comfortable and joyous. Group songs, solo songs, mimics and so on added to the entertainments. The food, drinks and snacks were also good. At certain stations the train had long halts. Sometimes we walked on the platforms or went to the tea and coffee stalls and got refreshed. We reached the New Delhi junction at 8.30 am. The tourist bus arranged by our college authority was lying in the parking lot ready to help us. We all got in the bus which carried us to the hotel where we were going to stay for four days. We were given two big dormitories. We had our baths and got ready to go out to visit the Taj Mahal. It is regarded as the best example of Mughal architecture and a symbol of India's rich history. It attracts 7-8 million visitors a year and in 2007, it was declared a winner of the New 7 wonders of the world. It was built in 1648 by Shah Jehan as a memorial to his wife. We reached the Taj Mahal gate which is built in red sandstone. The very name of the monument is given in honour of Mumtaz Mahal, Shah Jahan the emperor's wife who died in childbirth. It is known as the monument of love and grieving emperor's ode to his beloved deceased queen. It is the jewel of Muslim art in India and one of the universally admired masterpieces of the world's heritage. The architecture of Taj Mahal has British, French, Mugal, Arabic and Hindu influences. Shah Jahan, the Mughal emperor built it over the grave of Mumtaz and later his grave was also erected beside it by his son Aurengazeeb. The main structure is constructed on a high platform. On each of the four corners of this platform there is a minaret ---the marble dome in the centre looks like an inverted lotus.

We entered through the main entrance. There is a red sand stone edifice outside the gate. The path leading to the mausoleum complex that houses the tomb of Mumtaz Mahal and Shah Jahan itself is a wonderful treat to the eyes of the visitors. The plants and the willow trees on either sides of the two roads and the wide and long water stored pool with the transparent reflection of the wonderous monument capture everyone's attraction. The interior of the mausoleum is organized around an octagonal marble chamber ornamented with low- relief carvings and semiprecious stones. Therein are the cenotaphs of Mumtaz Mahal and Shah Jahan. The Taj contains 120 rooms, a hall of mirrors and the pavilion, an elaborate fountain-like structure that stimulated the effect of rain. The Taj Mahal has four main iwans and twelve secondary ones, again twelve more on the floor. The graves are preserved in the basement and sealed. The visitors can walk around the balcony and watch the graves. Both the tombs are located in a dark room under the dome. Because of this monument Mumtaz Mahal became immortal. I add one more title to this monument:-

"The crown of India." It appeared that magnificent to me.

Shah Jahan spent all his money and time on making Taj Mahal. The monument is made with white marble stone and inside it there are various designs made up of glass which depicts the love between the emperor and his wife. The selection of the location is noteworthy:- near the bank of river Yamuna, in Agra, Uttar Pradesh, North India. It is the effort of 20,000 workers for 22 years. It was made with hands and its beauty determines the magic and splendor of ancient architects. Sad to say after the construction the hands of Ustad Ahamad Lahori, the architect who made it were cut off so that he wouldn't have constructed another one like this. Although emperor Akbar was the most renowned Mughal emperor, Shah Jahan became world famous in connection with one of the seven wonders of the world.

Our next day's visit was to the Red Fort. It is the palace fort of emperor Shah Jahan's capital Shahjahanabad. It is famous for its massive enclosing walls reflecting the fusion of Islamic, Persian, Timurid and Hindu styles. It is a place of major tourist attraction. This red sandstone stone walls stand twenty three meters high encircling a complex of palaces, entertainment halls projecting balconies, baths and indoor canals and gardens as well as an ornate mosque. It was the main residence of the emperors of the Mughal dynasty. None other than Shah Jahan commissioned the construction of this historic fort in Agra, Old Delhi on the bank of river Yamuna, the design of which is again credited to Ustad Ahamed Lohori who constructed the Taj Mahal. It is Delhi's most iconic monument that spreads over 255 acres of land. Its significance and centre of attraction is enhanced by the fact that every year on India's Independence Day the Prime Minister hoists the country's flag here.

The Red Fort houses a large number of museums, public audience hall, Diwan-i-aam, Diwan-i-Khas, Moti Masjid, mosque and palaces.

The Mumtaz Mahal is one of the six main palaces situated facing the Yamuna River. Rang Mahal is the palace where the emperors' wives and mistresses were housed. The public audience hall was a location for receptions where Shah Jahan received courtiers and state guests. Moti Masjid is built at the highest point. This pearl mosque sits on a platform and consists of a large courtyard surrounded by continuous arcades and a prayer hall built as a place of worship for the royal members of the court. The structure contains three huge domes of high architecture value. The Diwan –i-am is a huge Hall of Audience where the Mughal emperors received the public and heard their grievances. We saw the prison room where the World Renowned Shah Jahan The Mughal emperor was imprisoned by his own cruel son Aurengzeb from where the former used to watch The Taj mahal till he died.

Our next day's visit was Kutub Minar. It is a 73 m high tower built in 1193 AD by Qutab –ud-din Aibak. It is the tallest brick minaret in the world built with five storeys and projecting balconies. The 379 stairs inside the tower lead to the top. Forty five visitors most of them students died in a stampede inside the minar on December 4, 1981. Its pillar is not rusted because it was made by 98% wrought iron and the absence of sulphur/ magnesium is the reason for its longevity. Inside the minar there is a mosque, a rust proof iron pillar and a domed gateway to the mosque. Though we visited certain other places too, The Taj Mahal, the Red Fort and The Kutub Minar are the ones that captured my memory even to this day. It was time for us to return to our college and hostel.

The college authorities were in a hurry to finish the portions of the syllabus as the close of the last semester was fast approaching. Side by side the sports day and the college anniversary were also to be done with. Though I had not attended any coaching in sports I was very much interested in different sports items. Soon after the classes in the college and study hours in the hostel my friends and I were in a hurry to go for short outings around within the time limits permitted. Glad to say I could stand first in long jump, high jump, discus throw and obstacle race. So everybody in the college knew who Francis Lucas was. I was good at singing though never attended music class. Out of sheer taste and interest I learned a Telugu film song from a recent Telugu movie. When I felt sure that I could sing it before the audience I gave my name to the college anniversary celebration organizer. He was more than happy to accept me after listening my song. Thus my mind was not for studies but for sports competitions and annual college function. With enthusiasm even today I recall the great applause I got from the audience for my Telugu song. All the extracurricular activities of the year were over and the annual public examination was fast approaching. Many were getting serious about studies but though I wanted to, I could not bring myself to that. Actually it was my wish that I should finish my degree to get selected for a good rank in the police department. Even at my middle age now I regret that I didn't do justice to my own career selection. As it was compulsory to study sitting in the study hall I could not but study from 7 pm to 10 pm and 6 am to 9 am, in between there was dinner in the evening and breakfast in the morning each taking half-an-hour respectively. On Saturdays and Sundays we were free to go or do anything we liked provided we did the studies at the scheduled hours. On every week, these two days I had expensive and sumptuous lunch with my friends as the hostel meals were often tasteless. Each time I had food in the restaurant I remembered my friend Peter Antony who was the cause of my having pocket money. Days, weeks and months passed by. The month of exam- April dawned. I started becoming serious about the examination and so with my studies. The following two weeks and the ten revision holidays I became buried in my books. I found no time for any kind of outings, arguments or quarrels. I was ok with the hostel food. My only concern was my annual public examination. So I made the full advantage of my study hours and leisure times.

I made thorough study of selected chapters, topics and essays. When the exams were over I felt that I would get through and when the results were out I barely passed and that was happy enough for me. Without leaving any subject or paper in pending I could start the second year. My parents, siblings and more than all I was very happy that I passed the 1ˢᵗ year fully.

I repeated the same routine activities in the 2ⁿᵈ year too. Many of my friends who were hardworking all through the year could not get through all the subjects. So my happiness knew no bounds. I was proud of my performance in the examination as my Malayalee friends Sebastian Thottam and Abhilash Mathew each had to recover some papers of the first year. Thus I was overjoyed when the result was published. But my outings, eating in the restaurants and so on went on as before. Like the previous year I concentrated on my studies towards the end of this year as the exams were nearing. Sebastian Thottam's father Joseph Thottam was the owner and manager of a primary school in Guntur where his house was. One evening when Sebastian, Abhilash and I were sitting together and gossiping, by chance the topic of our annual examination came up. Sebastian, "If we don't pass in all subjects in 1ˢᵗ year and 2ⁿᵈ year we will lose one year. Unless we get through it fully we cannot join the degree course, nursing school or any good course. I will work in my father's school and simultaneously study and prepare to recover the failed subjects."

I, "as I am slack and reckless in my studies all through the year I doubt if I will pass in all subjects this year. So will your dad accommodate me as a teacher under him? Otherwise how can I spend one whole year in my house? I am really scared."

Abhilash, "I am not scared to be at home but it will be a boredom. It will be fun if we three can work in the school as teachers till we can join some other course."

I, "Sebastian, what do you think about our programme for one year? Will your father agree?."

Sebastian, "I think there is a possibility. I will present the matter to my father. Every year teachers come and go in our school as it is not a government recognized or aided one which can afford good payment to the teachers and so they go in search of better pastures."

I, Sebastian, take it for granted that I will be ready even if the pay is less."

Abhilash, "be sure I will also go by the conditions your father puts."

Sebastian, "It is a residential school, food and accommodation will be free added to the salary which the school provides you."

A sigh of relief from inside of me. Otherwise what would I do for one year in case I don't get through the intermediate course fully. It was my great ambition that I should earn a job in the police department as Sub Inspector for which I had to get a degree certificate and then apply in the PSC. I was physically fit, I evaluated myself, but I had to pass the intermediate exams and then get a degree. In my fancy and imagination I was working as a police officer controlling and punishing the culprits and making them obey me. I had high esteem for my imagined abilities and smartness to handle culprits and wrong doers. But I was too lazy to put my efforts and energy and time to study. Then how could I quench my aspiration!. During the study hours and revision holidays I was imagining to be a police officer. At the same time I was fancying myself as a teacher in the primary school for one year. I did not utilize the study time as I did for the first year exams. Once the public examinations were over Sebastian, Abhilash and I sat and talked again seriously about our plans and Abhliash and I went back to Kerala and Sebastian to his home in Guntur. Even before we made all these plannings Abhilash and I had been to Sebastian's home and their school, Oasis English Medium School as Sebastian had invited and taken us to spend the Dasara holidays with them. So we were not strange candidates to Mr. Joseph Thottam, the father of Sebastian when he mentioned us to his father. His school was running in loss and was unable to afford fully qualified and trained teachers. When the school closed for summer vacation two teachers had already submitted their resignation letters. So Joseph Thottam was happy to get two teachers for his school giving low salaries. When I heard about Mr. Joseph's reaction to our plan I was very happy. I don't know whether I wanted to work as teacher for one year or I wished to pass in all the papers and continue to study. I recall that I preferred to fail. I was under the yoke of regulations and rules at home, college and hostel. I wanted to be law maker in a classroom and make my pupils obey me. Under Mr. Joseph Thottam's premises I would be free and on my own after my work. I was going to be happy and free whether I pass or fail in the intermediate examination.

Luckily or unluckily I got the message from Sebastian by the middle of May that all three of us did not get through the exam. The news made me a bit sad which I could overcome in no time. Sebastian suggested that Abhilash and I could reach his place as early as possible to have a fun time before the school reopens for the new scholastic year. My father wouldn't be angry with me for failing in the intermediate course as he himself was not always good at his studies and had always pending papers every year. So he could understand me unlike my mother who was always top scorer in all the examinations. My brother and sister also could not take my failure as they both were very studious and top ones. Though younger to me they blamed me for failing.

Both Abhliash and I wanted to go soon, more than him I as I had lots of mental affiliations due to my father's verbal abuses, sometimes even bodily ones for no serious mistakes at all. That was my fate. It took only one week for us to go. We got our bags ready and started. From Vijayawada we took the bus to Guntur. It took us one hour and fifteen minutes to Guntur bus station and from there to the Oasis school in a rickshaw. We reached our destination in fifteen minutes. The owner and manager of the school Mr. Joseph Thottam, his wife and the office clerk

Mrs. Celine Thottam, their son and our friend and benefactor Sebastian Thottam hurried to the rickshaw. Mr. Joseph felt his hand in the pocket and before we did he disposed of the rickshaw driver paying his charge. We were warmly welcomed to their residence adjacent to the school building. Sebastian showed us into rather a large room that was allotted to both Abhilash and me. He asked us to have our shower and then to lunch. The room and the toilet were good enough for us. We had quite a sumptuous dinner after which three of us together arranged our things and beds. Sebastian, "as you know this is a residential school and we all will have the same food." (We were walking behind him and he as directing us to the kitchen of this house). "This is our kitchen, kitchen for five of us. From the hostel mess our food will be brought to our dining room and we eat here. If we help my mum in cooking we can make any food which can be added to the mess food of our share. My father will take care of buying any food item which we are willing to cook if we want extra." I, "That sounds good. We three can help your mum or do even independent cooking when we feel like."

Abhilash, "That is good, we won't get bored with hostel food."

Sebastian, "no worries for anything, as dad is a very co-operative and benevolent one." After seeing the accommodation and the facilities without even taking a rest I wanted to see the classroom, its facilities and the campus around. So I said,

"Come on, let us go around this place and see everything."

Abhilash, "Why in a hurry now? We have seen the place once, don't you remember?."

I, "That was just casual and random. At that time I never thought that I will become a teacher here (we were walking through the school assembly ground and entering the classrooms).

I continued, "I stand in the middle of the class, walk around the class, sit and mark the attendance of the students, teach them and ask them questions. Friends, I feel I am floating in the air-the students get up from their seats to wish me. Wonderful. For the first time I am going to be somebody. They will be paying attention to what I say. That night all three of us slept in the same room. We talked for a long time before we retired to bed. The next morning by 8 am Sebastian told Abhilash and me that we were to be in the school office at 10 am. We both were called before Mr. Joseph Thottam at the same time. After the formal greeting to each other Mr. Joseph said:-

"You both are going to be first time teachers now. Though you are going to handle and manage a primary class your responsibility is not simple. You have to maintain discipline in the class room first and foremost. The working hours are from 9 am to 3 pm and you must handle all the subjects, you will have one free period a day which is allotted to Telugu. The physical education teacher will take care of one period a week, and you are free that period too. You have to do everything you can to promote the all-round development of your class, for which you can utilize the weekly cultural activity period. This is all about your responsibilities. Now comes the salary part. You are given free boarding and lodging here. Added to that I will pay you Rs 500 as your monthly pay. I will also meet your travelling fare to Kerala and return for two vacations. If my conditions are accepted, both of you are appointed." "I am Ok." Both Abhilash and I said in one accord immediately. Smiles spread on three faces.

Mr. Joseph Thottam, "Not fine, very good."

He continued, "Tomorrow is Saturday. Shall we five make a day's trip to Nagarjuna Dam?"

Again in one voice it sounded and echoed,

"Oh ! Yes, sure".

It was a day's journey and we all got ready for the next day's trip. We were in a small van and so had enjoyed the journey. We reached the station at 7 in the morning. It is the world's largest masonary dam protected with 26 gates. Nagarjuna Dam is located in Nalgonda district, built across River Krishna. It has the irrigation capacity for 9.81 lakh acres of land. The dam was formally inaugurated by the Prime Minister Jawahar Lal Nehru in 1955. The Nagarjuna Sagar Lake and Nagarjunakonda (hill) are all attractions. The museum and the wild life sanctuary attracted me the most. The Nagarjuna sagar lake is beautiful being the third largest manmade lake in the world. We went for a short boat ride in the lake. The famous and well-maintained museum houses, ancient artifacts were all lovely sights. As we had gone to Delhi and Agra tour from the college and seen so many wonderful sights this tour did not captivate me much. But we three enjoyed our travel and the time we had together without any botheration of studies and rules and regulations. More than everything I enjoyed and appreciated the generosity and goodwill of Mr. Joseph Thottam. I was always comparing my dad with him. He was like a friend to his son though Mr. and Mrs. Thottam had arguments and fights between themselves as he was often using alcohol. Sebastian and I became his friends in drinking in the weekends. Abhilash joined us some times. I must say sincerely that Mr. Joseph Thottam played an important role in my becoming an alcohol addict as I started the lesson there. Yet I cannot put the blame on him as Sebastian absolutely withdrew from alcohol and is now a teetotaller where as I am an addict to alcohol which is ruining my life now.

There were three more weeks for the school to be reopened. We three were to meet Mr. Joseph Thottam on Thursday. We entered the school office as asked. After a casual talk Mr. Joseph turned to Sebastian "You will be the teacher for Standard V A, you Francis you are in charge of Standard IV, division A and Abhilash, you take the responsibility of IV B division."

After that introduction he handed over the teacher's copy books to each of us of all the various subjects. Till the school reopened both Mr. and Mrs. Thottam were very busy in the school office with new admissions, collection of the first term fees and dealing with parents. We three were in our room just going through the books- the lesson titles, topics and so on. That night we had fun each of us pretending to be the teacher and the other two as students. We were making fun of each other's teaching and guiding each other too. Within this very short time we five were like a family. As both the older ones in the family were busy in the school office we three decided that after the breakfast we would take care of the kitchen preparing lunch and dinner till the regular hostel mess started. This was a good help to Mrs. Celine Thottam. Along with Sebastian we too went for kitchen shopping and then we did the cooking. Thus we were happily engaged and the days and the weeks flew by fast. Meanwhile we got the information that our marklist was ready in our college and none of us was happy to get that information. Any way we had to go and collect it before the school started functioning and so we did it in time. I had failed in two papers, Sebastian had to recover one paper of the 2nd year and two pending papers of the 1st year, whereas Abhilash had two papers of each year. So apart from the school duties and responsibilities we had to find time to revise, study, mug up, rewrite the exams and pass. I made up my mind that I will do justice to my work and studies.

Throughout the school working hours I was alert and conscious about my position and status as the teacher before my students. Before I went to bed I made sure that I prepared my lessons well so that I will not be blank about the portion. Every day I gave them dictation, home work and monthly tests. Classroom discipline was well-maintained yet my students were free and friendly with me. Very soon I knew my students by name and face. After the preparation for the next day's classes, I took keen interest in my studies too. Abhilash and Sebastian were good and responsible teachers. I took enough attention in the extra-curricular activities of these primary school children. I trained them in action songs and performing playlets. I was finding fun in my job as the students and the headmaster appreciated me. My desire was that after the 1 year of teacherhood and passing of intermediate I should secure a graduation in degree so that I could secure a good job in the police department. Some of my friends in Kerala who passed PDC (Predegree course, equivalent to intermediate) joined the School of Nursing. Till that time only girls went for this course and became nurses. Male nursing was becoming a craze as it promoted foreign jobs. Very soon I changed my long-cherished ambition to nursing. Abhilash too seemed interested in nursing after listening to me. With a new enthusiasm and energy I started my studies to complete and pass the Intermediate course and the result was that I passed the Intermediate Course with good marks.

Everyone at home was happy about my success. As it was in the initial start many boys wanted to get seats in nursing school. From my friends I came to know about Damien School of Nursing in Bangalore. Any how I took a liking for that institution, the name Damien attracted me as I had heard about Fr. Damine's service. When I told my parents about my liking for nursing course my father was against it as he wanted me to become a more prestigious person than a nurse. But as I was so persistent about it, he finally agreed. Admission was open to any candidate who passed PDC or its equivalent and ready to pay the donation amount along with the first year college fees and hostel fees. No doubt there was a formal interview which did not matter much. So we were in a hurry to reach the institution before the admission was closed. So my father got ready in a couple of days and we went to Bangalore. There was nothing tuff about the interview. After a few friendly questions I was showed to the owner and manager's office room where my father was seated when I underwent the name's sake interview. The money matters were cleared and I was given the admission card which I had to submit in the office on the day of commencement of the course and we were dispersed. We went around the campus and the hostel and it was all quite good. Inside the Damien School of Nursing boundary itself there was another building and we were told that it was yet another nursing school the name of which was very inspiring –Florence Nightingale School of Nursing. We could guess that it was for women. Their hostel was a separate building with independent compound walls. All these four institutions were owned by one and the same person. Mr. Jagadish Chandra Gupta who is a physical MD but now working in his own nursing schools after his twenty five years of service in Anandapur Medical College. To me Dr. Jagadish was a hero ready for risky undertaking. He seemed adventurous to me. His input in his elaborate scheme was huge and so he had to levy it from the candidates from different forms like donation, fees and hostel fees. I thought:- "Once I become a full-fledged nurse I must do something to make money at any cost." Thus we got some idea about the nursing school, its facilities, hostel and its facilities and the surroundings. Happily we returned home. My mother and siblings were eagerly wiring for our return to hear everything.

One day I overheard my father telling my mum.

"Actually I didn't like our Francis's idea of selecting his career as a nurse. But now I feel that I am on his side. He is more like me than he is like you. I took twelve years to pass my schooling of ten years. He is better than me and did it in ten years. To get through my PUC (Pre University Course) I made three attempts but Francis did only two. For my degree I made three reexams. Any way nursing is easier than a degree course and career oriented too. I think Francis made a good selection of his own."

Lucy, "I too think so. In three years he will earn his living and become independent."

Hearing their conversation I became excited. When we were having our evening tea together I said,

"Dad, before going to the nursing school as you know I must have white pants and shirts, shoes and socks and so on."

Dad, "I was just thinking about that. Ok, tomorrow we all will go to the textile shop and buy the things."

Only on very rare occasions my dad used to talk gently and friendly to me. Any way I had no tender feelings towards him.

Even when he was good and soft, old and bad dealings poped up into my mind as sad experiences were printed in my brain. The very next day after the breakfast my dad, mum, Elsa, Joe and I started to the shopping centre. I had taken the four wheeler licence when I was working as a teacher in Oasis School. Everyone in the family had known that. On the way I asked my dad to let me drive the car for some distance. I saw the three of them sitting at the back seats looking at each other in confusion.

Stephen answered cooly :"No, Francis. Be patient. Later…….."

I interrupted, "Why not now? I have licence, you know that."

Francis, "How did you get the licence!." I, "like anybody else, I got after going for driving classes, practicing and passing the tests."

Francis, "Who paid for it?."

I, What a question dad? I did it while I was working as the teacher. You know everything and keep asking questions."

Francis, "So earn a job, make money, buy a car and then drive."

I, "For that do I need your permission?."

Lucy, "Francis, son don't argue and fight. He is driving don't distract him."

I became very angry and said,

"Dad, stop the car. I will get down and come to the textile store by bus. What kind of a father you are?."

Elsa, "Brother, please be good. I'm on your side but avoid problem."

Joe, "I say the some thing to you."

Anyway I was angry but stopped the arguments and fights.

Once we entered the store the two of us behaved like gentlemen. Four pairs of white trousers and shirts, one pair of nurses' coats, socks were all selected very soon. Then Stephen told me to select what I wanted other than the uniform outfits. I was glad to hear that and selected two more pairs. Elsa and Joe made their selection too. After that two pairs of white shoes were also bought. We went home after having lunch in a good restaurant. Though I was happy with the shopping I didn't like to sit next to the driver. I asked my mother to take the seat near him in front and I sat with my siblings. We were having fun together cracking jokes and singing. After reaching home I put on my nurse' uniform and appreciated myself in the mirror. I pretended to be the nurse's and treated my siblings and mum as my patients and had a nice time again. My dad's words were ringing in my ears and I said to myself:-

"I must buy a vehicle of my own. Car is too expensive, but I must buy a motorbike."

I reached my institution- Damien school of Nursing one week early. I was showed into a room a four bed room one and was asked to select any bed and I did the one in a corner beside the window. After I settled down in the room and had my food I went around to see around the place thoroughly. The hostel mess hall and the kitchen were separate buildings inside the compound wall. The mess hall was almost empty as the school did not start functioning. While I was having my lunch I happened to meet the head cook who was a Malayalee. From him I came to know that there were a handful of vacancies still left in my school and in the Florence Nightingale School. Anyone who could bring a candidate would be given a good sum as commission. This was a very energizing idea. Immediately Abhilash Mathew came to my mind. I remembered him saying once when we were in Oasis School that a nurse is one who is qualified to work anywhere in the world. Without wasting any time, I contacted Abhilash giving all the details. He seemed indecisive. When my dad's friend came to know about my admission in Damien's School of Nursing and about the Florence Nightingale one, he got interested to get a seat for his daughter. This gentleman Mr. Peter Savio had seen me along with my dad two or three times.

Our hostel warden informed me that I had visitors and they were Mr. Peter Savio and his daughter. After the talk for a short while I took them to the Principal and introduced them referring to my dad and myself. After the formal interview with the candidate and discussion with the father she was admitted in the   nursing school and hostel. That very evening I was called to the office and was given a good sum as my commission. This was my stepping stone to buy a motorbike. My anxiety stole half of that nights' slumber and so I got up late that morning. To my great surprise there stand Abhilash Mathew and his dad at the door step of my bedroom. All three of us were very happy. Together we went for breakfast and then to the principal by 10.15 am. After the usual procedure Abhilash was admitted. The commission added to my sum for the purchase of motorbike. Abhilash and I were in the same room and so we both were happy to go about the new place. There were only three more days left for the nursing schools to start functioning. For both the schools it was the fourth batch of the nursing course. The principal's room, office and the hostels were all busy and rushy with old students and new candidates. The first week of the first year nursing was good and interesting. As I was inquisitive I came to know that there were vacancies in male and female sections. Peter Antony who was my friend and boss in seizing cars promised that he would see to it that he gets candidates for me and get a share in the commission. Before the close of the second week of my course four newcomers came to me as directed by Peter Antony two each to the male and female sections at different hours. I handled the matters deligently and Peter was pleased too. Classes, practical works and studies at nights were all going on without any rest. Though busy with the various activities related to the course, I was doing everything with great interest. I was very good at my practicals as I was interested. I liked the lectures on anatomy and physiology the most. But on the whole the nursing training and studies are hard. Lot to learn, challenging exams, complicated schedules and the assignments are hard experiences. Even though many of my friends failed in certain papers I managed to pass the 1st year exam fully.

Five of us including Abhilash Mathew and me moved from the hostel to an adjacent apartment for more freedom and less monthly expenditure. I got the one year hostel fees from home and what I could save added to my collection to buy the motorbike. One day a youngster by name Jerald Periera from the nearby apartment invited us for his birthday celebration where we were offered pale ale beer, and beef curry along with food. Gradually Jerald Periera and I became friends, close friends and intimate friends. We both gave each other company in drinking and outings on weekends. I always felt that I was an ignored member in my family. When I was in Oasis School, I felt I was important. When I was in the company of Paul James seizing cars for the money lenders I felt my importance again. With Jerald Periera I was becoming important again. Here all I was listened to, my suggestions were taken and appreciated and never reproached and rebuked. One day I told Jerald Periera about my desire to buy the same brand motorbike. Suzuki Samurai which the latter was using. Jerald wanted to help me. As it was the kind of job which he himself was doing he explained me how to do it, its merits and demerits, anxieties and risks. After listening to all that he said, I said:-

"Jerald, my dear I am for it as far as it doesn't hinder my studies. I want to own a motorbike of my own which I can use only with my permission."

Jerald, "I didn't get what you meant."

I, "Forget it, that's it."

Jerald, "You say I'm your best friend…"

I, "Ok-Ok. My father doesn't permit me to use his car or scooter. I was angry about it and so undeliberately I expressed it."

Jerald, "Do justice to your studies and assignments. Allot your time for this work on weekends."

I, "OK"

Together we went to a liquor store known to Jerald. The deal was that on every Friday in each fortnight the store would sell me two packs of twenty four bottles each, one containing Pale ale and the other Old Monk with the price of fifty rupees each bottle. The bottles were inserted in the empty spring water cardboard boxes to avoid checking of the squad. To sell these items in Kerala I took the help of Peter Antony who was my friend and leader in seizing vehicles for the money lenders. Peter Antony had to find out stores or people who would buy the stuff that I would bring for rupees two hundred and fifty each bottle. I bought two leather bags to carry each cardboard box. My train to Kerala was at 7 pm. On Friday after the class I went to the store, collected the two packs, packed them in my leather bags and went to the railway station. I got in the general compartment, placed my bags under the seat and occupied the seat opposite to my bags. I was the first passenger to get in. I didn't sleep at all as my anxiety and fear haunted me. The swaying of the seat did not sooth me to slumber. With whistles, horns, howls and roars the train hurried to its destination. On Saturday by 9 am I reached my location. Peter Antony was pacing with the train on the platform as it was slowering, peeping into each general compartment. Seeing him I waved and screeched out of joy and enthusiasm. The train hardly came to standstill than Peter reached and carried one bag and we got out of the station. The taxi was waiting for us and Peter directed the driver. We reached a liquor store and entered in. This store had three more branches. Both the cardboard boxes were taken by the owner of the store and then and there paid the whole. I was relieved of all my worries. We went to a restaurant and had good food. In the other business Peter Antony used to pay me and from now on it was my turn to pay. His service was good and essential and I paid him well. He had taken a reservation ticket for me to return. Happily I started my way back. I slept well on berth peacefully and comfortably as I had no sleep the previous night. I was driving a Suzuki Samurai in my sleep. I reached my apartment in the morning. Jerald Periera was aware of the time I would come and he was glad to learn that my operation alco went well and smooth. Carrying out this operation all through the year enabled me to make money to buy Suzuki Samurai bike.

The 2nd year nursing exam was fast approaching. After the daily written assignments I was devoting no less than two hours mugging up topics and lessons in connection with the examination and I could do well and got through all the papers. In the intervening period of vacation and commencing of the course I joined Peter Antony in seizing vehicles for the money lenders. When the 3rd year started I took the hostel fees for one year from my father. I went about with my friends and did what I liked. There was no open fight or physical abuse, but cold wars from different directions between Stephen and me. All his conversations were offensive and insultive.

Before the classes started I reached Bangalore. Jerald Periera and I went to four motorcycle dealers to check my favourite brand Suzuki Samurai and find out which dealer was the most favourable and finally fixed on one. After finishing all the formalities I took it to apartment and my joy knew no bounds. For several weeks on end I roamed about every nook and corner of the city and became familiar with every part of Bangalore, its lanes, stores, markets and shopping centers.

On one Saturday morning I went to the Lal Bag Botanical Garden of Bangalore. I wanted to be all alone as I liked to be alone and didn't want any one directing or prompting to go here or there. When I was going around the different places inside the glass house my eyes caught sight of a loney girl who was wandering about paying attention to nothing but seemed deep in thought. At the very first sight a feeling of attraction towards her ensnared me. Her charming face, long and thick hair and her elegant walk like the peahen's strutting diverted my mind from the haunts of my embarrassed situation at my home to a pleasant mood. Though I was following her whereever she walked into and looking at her overall elegance she understood nothing of that.

I said to myself, "I came here friendless, so too she is. Even here I am moody, so too she is, she is beautiful and charming and I am no less handsome or smart. But I have anguishes abound and she seems to be in untold ails, and so something all in common."

My mind was a bit distracted from her and she was no more in that spot. With a slight panic I looked around and luckily for me saw her going out and waisting no time I followed her. She was walking to the park right in front of the glass house and I was a stone throw away distance from her. I was happy that she sat on a bench and without hesitating I took a seat on the nearby bench. As soon as I sat her eyes reached me. I smiled heartily and she forced out one stretching her lips stingily. I was happy even for that and slowly walked towards her and even before reaching her.

I said, "Hai"

Giving a better smile she said, "hello"

I, "Are you from Kerala?"

She, "Why did you think so?."

I, "You look so."

She, "Yes, I am. And you?."

I was happy about this question and said, "I too"

I, "May I know your name please?."

She, "Good or bad my name is Dora Augustine. As everyone calls me Dora you too can. I am from Alleppy. Here I am doing my nursing course in Service Shower School of Nursing and I am in 3rd year. I think I gave you answers for all that you wanted to know of me. Didn't I?."

I,"Dora, I wonder why you show off as a tough one !. As I like your way and attitude let me copy you. I am Francis Lucas, I am from Ernakulam Dist. I study in Damien School of Nursing and am a 3rd year student. You wanted to snub my further questions or conversation. But I am different."

Dora, "Don't you know parallel lines never meet. So we must stop and go."

I, "I said I am different which means we are like opposite poles having some attraction. Again I have heard that friendship between opposite sex is very sincere as hate, jealousy and revenge find no room there."

Dora, "Can be. So far I never had and so I know not for sure."

I, "My situation is not different."

Dora, "Sounds good."

I, "So we both are the first time friends to each other of the kind." We exchanged looks and smiles at each other. I never thought it was that easy to get a girl as friend. I, "Dora, can I take the liberty to ask you a personal question?"

Dora, "By all means you can but to respond is my liberty."

I, "Ok Dora, why were you looking so preoccupied and gloomy while walking around the glass house?."

Dora, "Though I was walking around, I noticed you and your dissatisfactory face and negative outlook and expression on face though you look handsome and smart. What about that?"

I, "I asked you first.

So you answer first.

You asked after I asked.

So my answer will be after yours.

Sounds logical and reasonable?"

Dora, "Yes you are right. So, let both of us wait for the next meeting of ours to share our tales."

I said, "That's good"

Dora, "Francis, I am happy that I have a friend in you."

I, "The same here Dora"

Dora, "I think I must return to my hostel now."

Pointing to the restaurant I told her, Let's have a cup of tea and then go."

Dora, "Francis, as you please."

Together we went to the restaurant. She took a cup of coffee and I had a cup of tea. When she told me about the location of her nursing school and hostel I offered to drop her as that was on my way to my apartment. Reluctantly and timidly she agreed. With a pretty girl seated behind my seat proudly did I drive my bike along the road. After a short time of fifteen minutes Dora said;

"Francis, you can drop me here". I stopped and Dora got down. We looked at each other but said nothing. I broke the silence. "Dora, when are we going to meet again to share our stories?"

Dora, "Is the next Saturday OK with you?"

I, "No problem, I will make it. We will meet at the same place where we started our conversation today at 9 in the morning this coming Saturday."

Dora, "That's fine Francis."

From the time I parted from Dora I was thinking of her always. Her appearance, outside personality, manners, looks, talks and reservedness kept coming into my mind incessantly. We both were doing 3rd year nursing and I was very particular not to be behind her leaving any paper for another chance to be passed. So I took care to study the portions and given notes and taking immense care to do the assignments. All through my academic career this was   the time that I allotted and devoted my most earnest endeavour and efforts to studies. It was Friday evening. During my night study and assignment I was distracted thinking about the next day. I was excited and thrilled about meeting her and spending time together. With regard to appointments with my parents, relatives and friends I had been always far from being punctual. I was not going to be so with Dora. My feelings towards her was so ardent that I reached the appointed place a little after 8.30 am. I sat on the garden bench impatient as I had to wait for half-an-hour. Aimlessly I looked around and caught sight of a girl wandering in the lawn. On a second glance I was astounded that it was none other than Dora. I was happy that we both were in the same boat. It was clear that she was interested in me. I hurried to her and she to me. We sat on the garden bench. I, "Why did you come half-an-hour early?."

Dora, "I ask you the same question:-

Why did you come early?"

I, "We know each other's answer I guess. I'm sure it makes both of us happy. Hope everything will turn out good for our future."

Dora said shyly, "I too wish so, Francis." We looked at each other and smiled.

I, "Dora, last week you told me that you will tell me the reason for your gloomy mood. Tell me what makes you sad." Sharing problems with a friend, be sure, will alleviate one's pain."

Dora was casting her eyes down, elbows on her knees and chin resting in the palms, face grim and upset when I asked. She sat motionless without even looking at me.

I, "Dora, I understood that you are not willing to tell me. I will never more ask you about it. I am a different one:- I actually like to tell you of my family problems as you became my dear friend".

Dora, "Francis, thank you for telling me what you take me to be. Don't tell me of your problem before I tell you mine. Let me postpone it for next week."

I, "As you like Dora."

I wanted to make her happy as she was looking moody. Together we walked aimlessly giving company to each other. We reached a meadow. We sat on the lawn and started talking.

Dora, "Francis, why did you select the career of a nurse? Usually men don't like this profession."

I, "Dora there is actually two reasons why I select it. Both my reason have equal importance to me. Many of the job oriented studies and courses are long-term ones. No doubt if I am willing and studious my parents would have accomplished their part to enable me achieve my ambition and goal though my father was miserly often. Yet for the benefits of his kids' future he would find money. Yet he wanted to be a dictator particularly as far as I am the subject. I wanted to be a despot wherever I am involved. General nursing is only a matter of three years. As male nurses are very few, opportunities are open wide. As these two reasons are interlinked I chose this profession. Certain incidents in my life keep popping up in my memory and mind often and they mainly laid the base for my selection of this branch of career line. I will just tell shortly to you so that you really understand why I want to be an earning member soon.

1. When I was below thirteen I was stripped off my clothes except for my panties by my father and was beaten from shoulder to feet with his belt which left bruises and scars all over my body.

2. When I was fourteen I was beaten with cow's rope from waist to feet for being late to bring the cows home as I was playing cricket with friends.

3. May be I was fifteen and on my way to school in the crowdy and rushy bus my lunch packet was dropped down and someone stepped on it and trampled underfoot. In the evening as I started my missed lunch my father snatched it and threw it away saying it was not lunch time, without giving me a chance to say what had happened in the bus.

4. I was made to sleep on the kitchen floor as I refused to take bath at 10.30 pm as I had it in the morning. He was

stubborn that I should take bath drawing water from the well.

Dora, these are only a few incidents which knock at the door of mind often. I'm sure such occurrences in the house make my mother excuse all my rebellious ways and ill-talks and treatments to her. As I am ashamed of myself I don't tell you or anyone how I treat and talk to my mother:- I'm out of control but she is sufferer with me."

Dora, "Francis, this is too much for any boy to bear. You are a hero. With a matured mind and thinking, take challenge and make a life for your happiness. But if you fail to make a life for you no one will blame your father but you. Remember :-

'Man is what he makes himself and not what education or environment make him'. Anyway you are prepared to be a nurse. You will find a job anywhere in the world and anywhere you go. So you and I have made apt choice, I guess. My little advice to you- there are many abandoned children who do odd jobs at the railway stations, bus stations, market places and so on to earn daily bread and later when they grow to be teenagers and adults they create jobs for themselves as small scale food stall owners, toys and dolls sellers, drivers, farmers, carpenters, masons, electricians and plumbers. Anyway they made you a nurse who can be a good earning member. So forget the painful past and take courage. Tell me about your brother and sister. How are you to them? How are they to you?." I, "Right younger to me is my sister Elsa Lucas. She is clever and studious devoting all her time to study. My mother does not tax any work from her except a very little. Dad too never interferes with her. She is a good one unlike me. I was jealous of her status and situation in the family and used to argue, fight and even beat her finding fault with her studies. She could only cry at my verbal and physical abuses. The same was my treatment towards my younger brother Joe Lucas. I used to be rude to them in the absence of my parents. My siblings were so scared of the possible aftereffects and so did not complain against me. I took advantage of that situation too. How I was treated, I paid back in the same coin towards my siblings and I felt pride that they were scared of me just as I was scared of my dad. Gradually I treated Elsa and Joe badly even in the presence of my parents. They could not resist my physical strength. So by and by all four were at a loss and I was enjoying my supremacy. Despite these situations I created for myself I was not really happy."

Dora, "Francis, how could you be all that I wonder !."

I, "Dora, I really don't know my own self. I suffered a lot, lot and lots under the dictatorship of my father. May be my ails, sufferings and withstanding moulded me to what I am now." We exchanged to each other the phone numbers of our hostels. I told Dora,

"Dora, shall we meet tomorrow in the same place at the same time?"

Dora, "Not tomorrow. I have lots to study and the assignments are in pending too. I am in a more hurry than you to finish nursing and earn a job. So I think we can meet on the coming Saturday".

I agreed, dropped her at her place and returned. Dora's earnestness about her studies and eagerness about securing the nursing certificate energised me further more about my goal. I thought that Dora and I should go to the Cubbon Park next week. On Sunday afternoon I called Dora on the hostel phone and asked her if she liked my idea and heard that she was quite happy. Though I offered to pick her from her place, she was not for that and offered to meet at the main gate of Cubbon Park which was hardly five kilometers from her hostel.

The classes, assignments and carrying out patients' care and services were done well along with my personal studies. Amidst my studies often I was lost in thought recollecting Dora's talks, jokes, advices, sober moods, appearance and what not !. Am I in her mind and heart as she is in mine? Even if not –let me think and take it for granted as 'Yes'. I was done with my scholastic works up to date by Friday night as I had to spend time with Dora on Saturday. I did not get good sleep that night pondering over all that I communicated with Dora the preceding week. I to myself:- "I was over in my talks. I knew her for some hours and revealed my things about my personal problems and my relations with family members. It was all awkard. It was all a shame. Sighs and pangs within me." On Saturday we met at the main gate of the park and together we went inside the park. Dora wanted to see around the Balbhavan Park. It has an area of 12.5 acres. There are hundreds of trees, playgrounds, a theatre and so on. In the toy train about 100 people can take a ride. There were many items of entertainments but both of us were not very keen about enjoying all that and so after some time we sat in the meadow. Dora, "Francis, after listening to your narration of the events in your family and your reactions I am really awestruck. For no reason you are rude and rough to your mother and siblings. I cannot understand that. Anyway, as a friend I tell you don't mess with your life. Now I am going to tell you a summary of my life so far and my ails. To begin with I am an orphan but adopted and having a foster father and mother. Do you like to hear more about me? Do you have an attraction or aversion towards me now? Whatever it may be I am continuing. Now I say of them as my parents. After five years of their marriage Mr. Martin Augustine and Mrs. Sofiya Augustin were not blessed with a baby. So they picked me from an orphanage at the age of one and raised me as their own. I was everything to them and they were everything to me. My father is a bus conductor and could earn only a meager salary. My mother bred and raised a few cows, goats and hens and made some income for the family. When I was four my mother gave birth to a baby girl and we three were very happy. After three years a baby boy was born too. Without any partiality or special care to any three of us our parents raised us and I felt no difference in my status in the house from the other two:- Lovely and Jerry. I was taking care of them while going to school, church or catechism classes and listened to me always. We loved each other like kins.

Our parents were finding difficulty in managing our needs, wants and minimum luxuries. They never asked me to become an earning member as a financial support to the family but I volunteered to be one after I finished my PDC. I sought the job for a teacher in any nursery school or lower primary school and finally I secured the position as a teacher in a lower primary school in Madras. I earned some extra income taking private tuitions too. I wanted to become a nurse but had to find out the fund for it. I saved all my tuition amount for that purpose and the rest was sent home for the family needs. Life went on like this for four years. My savings would not suffice my course. So I borrowed money from a priest, the head of a charitable institution on condition that I would pay them back as soon as I get a job and start working. Lovely fell in love with a boy and their marriage took place just three weeks ago and that was the reason I was looking desperate when you saw me. None of the four thought that I will be unhappy and develop a bad complex. I did not go home for Lovely's wedding. For the first time I felt that I don't belong there. I seriously think now that I don't belong or own anything there. My parents are for their younger kids and not for me but they utilized me. My studies and my future is my own responsibility."

For a few minutes we both remained quiet and sat lost in thought and then I broke the silence :-

"So, we both are the oldest of the kids in our respective families and thrown outs in one way or the other with some similarities and disparities."

Dora, "As seen we both are conditioned. I am shocked by your situations and no doubt you are by mine. I think we can stop for today and go to our residences after a cup of tea and coffee." We went to the restaurant had some refreshments, had some friendly talk and went our way without making any plan for the next visit.

I finished my nursing diploma and happy that I can get a job in Kerala, any part of India and anywhere in the world. I am indecisive about my future with regard to getting married and making a family for myself. This is a carefree life as a single, no responsibility, no worries, no misunderstanding and above all no arguments, quarrelling and no verbal or physical abuses.

www.ingramcontent.com/pod-product-compliance
Lightning Source LLC
La Vergne TN
LVHW091239180726
843490LV00006B/2120